CAMBRIDGE

AMERICAN EMPOWER

WORKBOOK
WITH ANSWERS

A1
STARTER

Rachel Godfrey

CONTENTS

1A I'M FROM MEXICO

1 GRAMMAR *be: I / you / we*

a Underline the correct words.

1 How are you / you are?
2 *I'm / I're* fine, thanks.
3 *You not are / You're not* in London.
4 *We're / We'm* from Brazil.
5 Where *am I / I am*?
6 **A** Are you OK?
   B No, *I not am / I'm not.*
7 **A** Are you a student?
   B Yes, *I am / I'm.*
8 **A** Are you from China?
   B No, *we's not / we're not.*

b Put the words in the correct order to make sentences and questions.

1 student / a / I'm .
   I'm a student.
2 teachers / not / We're .
   ____
3 from / I'm / not / Ecuador .
   ____
4 OK / Are / you ?
   ____
5 you / are / How ?
   ____
6 U.S. / the / we / in / Are ?
   ____

2 VOCABULARY Countries

a Find seven countries in the word snake.

b Complete the sentences with the country names. Use the letters in parentheses.

1 Rio de Janeiro is in Brazil. (r a b i l z)
2 Rome and Bologna are in ____________. (t i l y a)
3 Tokyo is in ____________. (n a j a p)
4 Quito and Guayaquil are in ____________. (r a u e d c o)
5 Bogotá is in ____________. (a l o m c o i b)
6 New York is in ____________. (s h u t e)
7 Barcelona is in ____________. (n i s p a)
8 Beijing and Shanghai are in ____________. (h a n i c)

3 PRONUNCIATION *I'm, we're*

a 01.01 Listen to the conversation. Complete the sentences.

A Hi. ____________ Horacio. What are your names?
B Hi. ____________ Carmen.
C And ____________ Camila.
A Nice to meet you. Are you from the U.S.?
B No, ____________ from Spain. ____________ Spanish.

1B HE'S ECUADORIAN

1 GRAMMAR *be: he / she / they*

a Complete the sentences with the words in the box.

is she   they're not   he's not   ~~are they~~   are   is   they are

1 Where __are they__ from?
2 **A** Are they Chinese?
  B Yes, __________.
3 **A** __________ they Italian?
  B No, __________. They're Spanish.
4 **A** __________ from Australia?
  B Yes, she __________.
5 **A** Is he Mexican?
  B No, __________.

b Complete the conversations with *is*, *'s not*, *'s*, *are*, *'re not*, or *'re*.

Conversation 1

A This [1] __is__ my friend Francisca.
B Where [2] __________ she from? [3] __________ she Brazilian?
A No, she [4] __________. She [5] __________ from Colombia.

Conversation 2

A Who [6] __________ Javier and Guillermo? [7] __________ they baseball players?
B No, they [8] __________. They [9] __________ soccer players.
A [10] __________ they American?
B No, they [11] __________. They [12] __________ Mexican.

c 01.02 Listen and check.

2 VOCABULARY Nationalities

a Complete the crossword puzzle.

→ Across

1 You're from the U.K. You're __British__.
2 She's from the U.S. She's __________.
3 He's from Australia. He's __________.
4 We're from Italy. We're __________.
5 You're from Ecuador. You're __________.
6 I'm from China. I'm __________.

↓ Down

1 He's from Brazil. He's __________.
7 They're from Spain. They're __________.
8 You're from Canada. You're __________.
9 We're from Japan. We're __________.

3 PRONUNCIATION Syllables

a 01.03 Listen to the words in the box. Complete the chart.

~~British~~   Colombian   Chinese   Italian   Brazilian
Canadian   Japanese   Spanish   American   Mexican

2 syllables	3 syllables	4 syllables
British		

1C EVERYDAY ENGLISH
Nice to meet you

1 USEFUL LANGUAGE
Meeting and greeting new people

a Underline the correct words to complete the conversations.

Conversation 1 (9 a.m.)

SELENA Good [1]*morning / evening*! How are you today?
AYLA I'm not [2]*bad / fine*, thanks. And [3]*you / are you*?
SELENA I'm [4]*nice / OK*, thanks.

Conversation 2 (3 p.m.)

HOLLY Good [5]*afternoon / evening*, Dean.
DEAN Hi, Holly. [6]*She / This* is my friend Natasha.
HOLLY Hi, Natasha. How [7]*you are / are you*?
NATASHA I'm good, [8]*thank / thanks* you.
Nice [9]*to meet / meet* you.

b 01.04 Listen and check.

c Complete the conversation with the words in the box.

and	~~good~~	hello	I'm	is	my
nice	thank	thanks	too		

CARLA [1] *Good* afternoon. [2] ________ name's Carla Ortega.
JAMES Hello. [3] ________ James Hargreaves.
CARLA [4] ________ to meet you, James.
JAMES Nice to meet you, [5] ________.
CARLA Oh, Aman! This [6] ________ James Hargreaves from Blue Web Technology.
AMAN [7] ________, James! How are you?
JAMES I'm fine, [8] ________ you. [9] ________ you?
AMAN I'm good, [10] ________.

d 01.05 Listen and check.

2 PRONUNCIATION Stressed words

a 01.06 Listen to the sentences. Which words are stressed? Check (✓) the correct box.

1 a [✓] How are you?
  b [ ] How are you?
2 a [ ] I'm fine, thanks.
  b [ ] I'm fine, thanks.
3 a [ ] So, this is your office.
  b [ ] So, this is your office.
4 a [ ] Good morning!
  b [ ] Good morning!
5 a [ ] I'm Andy and this is Ernesto.
  b [ ] I'm Andy and this is Ernesto.
6 a [ ] Nice to meet you.
  b [ ] Nice to meet you.

1C SKILLS FOR WRITING
I'm Italian

1 READING

a Read the personal profile and check (✓) the correct ending for the sentences.

Me and my friends

Hi. My name's Kurt Adler. I'm from Hamburg, in Germany. I'm a student in New York, in the U.S. My teacher is from Florida, in the U.S. My friends aren't from Germany or the U.S. Lia is from China, and Tamara is from Spain. Ana and Lucas are from Brazil.

1 Kurt is from … .
  a ☑ Germany
  b ☐ the U.S.

2 He's a student in … .
  a ☐ the U.S.
  b ☐ Germany

3 His teacher's … .
  a ☐ American
  b ☐ not American

4 His friends … .
  a ☐ are from Germany
  b ☐ aren't from Germany

5 Lia is … .
  a ☐ Japanese
  b ☐ Chinese

6 Tamara is from … .
  a ☐ Spain
  b ☐ the U.S.

2 WRITING SKILLS Capital letters and periods

a Underline the correct words.

Hello. [1]*my* / My name's [2]*alfonso* / *Alfonso*. I'm [3]*Italian.* / *Italian* My [4]*Friends* / *friends* are Nacho and [5]*Emma.* / *Emma* [6]*They're* / *they're* very nice. Nacho is from [7]*Spain* / *spain* and [8]*Emma.* / *Emma* is [9]*American.* / *American*

b Correct the sentences.

1 He's a student He's in your class.
He's a student. He's in your class.

2 This is diana
____

3 My teacher is canadian.
____

4 their apartment is in new orleans.
____

5 I'm from mexico.
____

6 We're American We're from Seattle.
____

3 WRITING

a Write a profile for you. Use Alfonso's profile to help you.

Hi! My name's ____________________

UNIT 1
Reading and listening extension

1 READING

a Read the email and match a–d to the parts of the email 1–4.

a ☐ saying goodbye
b ☐ Mark's new job
c ☐ greeting
d ☐ people in Mark's office

b Read the email again. Are the sentences true or false?

1 Trevor is in the U.S.
2 Mark is in Augusta, Maine.
3 Antonio is American.
4 Antonio and Cassidy are married.
5 Cassidy is a teacher.
6 Martin is from the U.S.
7 Yoko is from Japan.
8 Yoko is at home in the afternoon.

c Write an email to a friend about your new English class. Remember to say:

- where your class is
- who your teacher is and where he or she is from
- who the students are and where they are from.

Reply Forward

1 Hi Trevor,

How are you? How is Australia?

2 I'm great! My new job in Maine is good. The office is downtown in Augusta. Augusta is a great city! ☺

3 I'm in an office with three people – Antonio, Martin, and Yoko. Our office manager is Antonio. He's not American. He's from a small town in Mexico, but he's married to an American woman. Her name's Cassidy, and she's a teacher at a high school. Martin is British. He's from London, but his home is Augusta now. Yoko is Japanese. She's from Osaka. She's in the office from 8 a.m. to 1 p.m., and she's a student at an English school in the afternoon.

4 Say hello to your family for me!

Bye for now,

Mark

2 LISTENING

a 01.07 Listen to the conversation. Check (✓) the countries you hear.

Brazil	☐	Italy	☐
China	☐	Ecuador	☐
England	☐	Colombia	☐
Japan	☐	Spain	☐

b 01.07 Listen again and underline the correct words.

1 It is *morning* / *evening*.
2 Annie and Ben are *at home* / *at work*.
3 *Annie* / *Ben* is a new teacher.
4 Seattle is a city in *Washington* / *New York*.
5 Annie is from *Seattle* / *New York*.
6 Ben's class is *1A* / *1B*.
7 Daniela is an *Italian* / *Ecuadorian* student.
8 Simona and Gianna are *Spanish* / *Italian*.

c Complete the conversation with your own ideas.

A Good morning.
B Hi. Are you new?
A Yes, I am. My name's ____________.
B It's nice to meet you. I'm ____________.
A Nice to meet you, too.
B Where are you from?
A ____________, in ____________.
B Really? ____________'s a nice city.

Review

1 GRAMMAR

Correct the mistakes.

1 Cara aren't Chinese. She's American.
   Cara isn't Chinese. She's American.
2 **A** Where you are?
   B I'm in Barcelona.
3 I not am a student. I'm a teacher.
4 **A** And who this is?
   B This is Anton.
5 These are my friends. They Ecuadorian.
6 What your name?
7 We not Italian. We're Mexican.
8 Where Sue is from?

2 VOCABULARY

Check (✓) the sentences that are correct. Correct the mistakes.

1 ☐ They're from U.K.
   They're from the U.K.
2 ☐ She's Mexican.
3 ☐ He's from the Canada.
4 ☐ She's from the U.S.
5 ☐ We're Brasilian.
6 ☐ Are you Spainish?
7 ☐ I'm Japanese.
8 ☐ He's from Australia.

REVIEW YOUR PROGRESS

Look again at Review Your Progress on p. 14 of the Student's Book. How well can you do these things now?
3 = very well   2 = well   1 = not so well

I CAN ...	
say my name and country	☐
talk about people I know	☐
meet and greet new people.	☐

2A IT'S A BIG CITY

1 GRAMMAR *be: it's / it's not*

a Underline the correct words.

1 This is Santiago. *It's* / *He's* a big city in Chile.
2 This is my home. *It's* / *They're* a small apartment.
3 Nina's Russian. *It's* / *She's* from Vyborg.
4 The houses are new. *It's not* / *They're not* very big.
5 Adel is German. *He's* / *It's* from Berlin.
6 **A** Is Barcelona a small city?
B No, *it not* / *it's not*.
7 I'm from Göreme. *It's* / *She's* a town in Turkey.
8 **A** Are the apartments in the old part of town?
B Yes, *they are* / *it is*.

2 GRAMMAR Possessive adjectives

a Write the correct possessive adjective. Use the pronoun in parentheses to help you.

1 We're from London. ___Our___ (we) house is very old.
2 **A** What's ____________ (you) name?
B I'm Celine. I'm from Toronto.
3 Where's John? This is ____________ (he) book.
4 **A** They're from Mexico City.
B What are ____________ (they) names?
5 I'm Bruno. I'm from Italy, but ____________ (I) mother is Australian.
6 This is my friend. She's from China, and ____________ (she) name is Jia.

3 VOCABULARY Common adjectives

a Match the **bold** words with the opposite adjectives a–g.

1 [f] It's a **big** town. | a bad
2 [ ] This book is **boring**. | b easy
3 [ ] He's a very **good** soccer player! | c interesting
4 [ ] Why are they **happy**? | d old
5 [ ] This vocabulary is **difficult**. | e sad
6 [ ] Is your computer **new**? | f small
7 [ ] You're **right**. | g wrong

b Look at the pictures and complete the adjectives.

1 funny

2 r _ _ _ _

3 d _ _ _ _ _ _ _ t

4 _ oo _

5 h _ _ _ y

6 b _ a _ _ _ _ _ l

7 e _ _ y

8 b _ _ _ _ g

9 i _ _ _ _ _ _ t _ _ g

4 PRONUNCIATION Sound and spelling: /h/ and /w/

a 02.01 Listen to the words in the box. Which words have the /h/ sound? Which words have the /w/ sound? Complete the chart.

~~where~~ he what who his her hello when

/h/	/w/
	where

2B DO YOU HAVE A PHONE?

1 GRAMMAR Plural nouns

a Underline the correct spellings.

1 citys / cities
2 ticketes / tickets
3 watches / watchs
4 bottle of waters / bottles of water
5 knifes / knives
6 countries / countrys
7 boys / boyes
8 babies / babys
9 houses / housees
10 keys / keyes

2 GRAMMAR *I have / you have*

a Put the words in the correct order to complete the conversation.

JESSICA Oh, no!
TIMO What is it?
JESSICA My bag! It's at home!
TIMO Oh, no. [1]pen / you / have / a / do ?
Do you have a pen?
JESSICA No, I don't!
TIMO Here you are. [2]pens / two / I / have .
____
JESSICA Thanks.
TIMO And [3]you / a / dictionary / do / have ?
____
JESSICA Yes, [4]dictionary / have / a / I .
____
TIMO Good.
JESSICA Timo, [5]have / you / of / bottle / do / a / water ?
____
TIMO No, I don't. Sorry. But [6]I / apple / an / have !
____
JESSICA No thanks, Timo!

3 VOCABULARY Common objects 1

a Look at the picture and write the words.

1 a bag
2 a b__________
3 k__________
4 an u__________
5 a p__________
6 a b__________ of water

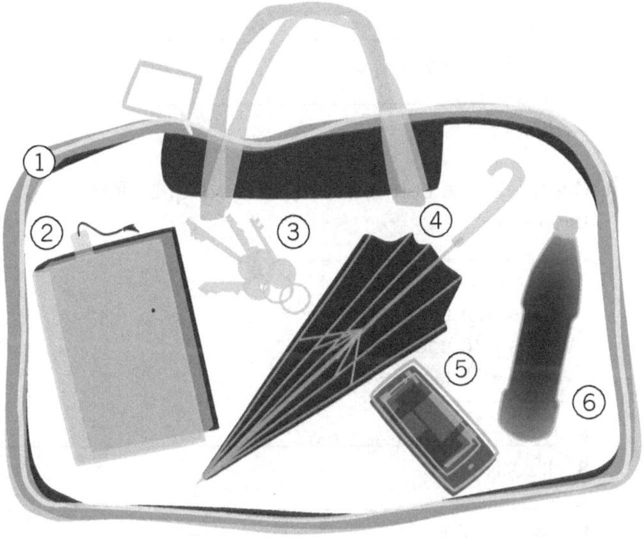

4 VOCABULARY Numbers 1

a 02.02 Listen and write the correct numbers.

1 I have eighty books.
2 __________ apples, please.
3 I have __________ bags.
4 __________ eggs, please.
5 Do you have __________ tickets?
6 __________ bottles of water, please.

5 PRONUNCIATION
Sound and spelling: /s/, /z/, and /ɪz/

a 02.03 Listen to the words in the box. Is the final sound /s/, /z/, or /ɪz/? Complete the chart.

~~knives~~ keys students newspapers
tickets books watches bottles houses

/s/	/z/	/ɪz/
	knives	

2C EVERYDAY ENGLISH
What's your address?

1 USEFUL LANGUAGE
Asking for and giving personal information

a Complete the questions. Use the letters in parentheses.

1 What's your __address__? (s d a d r e s)
2 How do you ______ that? (l s p l e)
3 What's your ______ ______? (o n m e n u p b e r h)
4 What's your ______ ______? (s e d m d a e i l a r s)
5 What's your ______ ______? (t i n r s a f e m)

b Complete the conversation with the questions in the box.

How do you spell that?
What's your phone number?
What's your address?
~~What's your last name?~~

A 1 __What's your last name?__
B It's Milner.
A 2 ______
B M-I-L-N-E-R.
A 3 ______
B It's 39 Oak Street, Buffalo, New York.
A 4 ______
B It's (716) 555-3214.

c 02.04 Listen and check.

d Complete the conversation.

A What's your 1 __last name__?
B 2 ______ Ramirez.
A 3 ______ do you spell that?
B R-A-M-I-R-E-Z.
A 4 ______ your phone number?
B 5 ______ (619) 555-9867.
A What's your email 6 ______?
B 7 ______ mramirez118@travelmail.com.

e 02.05 Listen and check.

2 PRONUNCIATION
Intonation in questions

a 02.06 Listen to the questions. Does the intonation go up (↗) or down (↘) at the end? Check the correct box.

	↗	↘
1 How are you?	☐	☑
2 Is it a small town?	☐	☐
3 What's your last name?	☐	☐
4 What's your address?	☐	☐
5 Can you spell that?	☐	☐
6 What's the spelling?	☐	☐
7 Are you from a big city?	☐	☐
8 Is this your phone?	☐	☐
9 Where are you from?	☐	☐
10 What's your email address?	☐	☐

2C SKILLS FOR WRITING
Vancouver's a great city

1 READING

a Read the information. Complete the form with the words in the box.

Stewart	American	Office
Gem	~~Kerry~~	745	9178

MONTY'S BOOK COMPANY

OUR PEOPLE

Hi. My name's Kerry Stewart. I'm from the U.S., but I live here in Canada. Vancouver's a great city, and I'm very happy here! My office is in the Gem Building on White Street. I'm in Room 745 with Kadim Baydar and Sandro Alessi. Our office phone number is 8969. My email address is kerryoz9178@travelmail.com.

First name:	1 Kerry
Last name:	2 ________
Nationality:	3 ________
Home address:	331 Ash Street, Apartment 2, Vancouver
Phone number:	(604) 555-1478
Office address:	Room 4 ________, The 5 ________ Building, White Street, Vancouver
6 ________ **phone number:**	8969
Email address:	kerryoz 7 ________@travelmail.com

2 WRITING SKILLS
The alphabet and spelling

a Underline the letter with the different sound.

1 A J K <u>R</u>
2 B C D F
3 M N G S
4 O Q U W
5 I X Y

b Correct the spellings.

1 bottel bottle
2 spel ________
3 eesy ________
4 fone ________
5 addres ________
6 toan ________
7 hapy ________
8 nashionality ________
9 offis ________
10 emale ________

3 WRITING

a Complete the form with information about you.

First name:	________
Last name:	________
Nationality:	________
Home address:	________ ________
Phone number:	________
Email:	________

UNIT 2
Reading and listening extension

1 READING

a Read the text. Check (✓) the correct summary 1–4.

1 ☐ Emily and Mark are married. They are managers in Seattle. They have a house in a town near Seattle.
2 ☐ Emily and Mark are married. They have a house in Seattle. Mark is a manager in a small town near Seattle.
3 ☐ Emily and Mark have a house in Seattle. They are receptionists in a big office in Seattle.
4 ☐ Mark is a receptionist in Seattle. He is married to Emily. They have a house in a town near Seattle.

b Read the text again. Check (✓) the correct answer.

1 Is Seattle a small town?
a ☐ Yes, it is.
b ☑ No, it's not.

2 Is Seattle rainy?
a ☐ Yes, it is.
b ☐ No, it's not.

3 Is it a boring place?
a ☐ Yes, it is.
b ☐ No, it's not.

4 Is Mark's office near an airport?
a ☐ Yes, it is.
b ☐ No, it's not.

5 Is Kenmore a big town?
a ☐ Yes, it is.
b ☐ No, it's not.

6 Is Emily and Mark's house new?
a ☐ Yes, it is.
b ☐ No, it's not.

7 Is their house near a supermarket?
a ☐ Yes, it is.
b ☐ No, it's not.

8 Is Mark happy?
a ☐ Yes, he is.
b ☐ No, he's not.

ABOUT

My name is Mark Smith, and I work in Seattle, Washington. Seattle is a big city with 700,000 people. It's rainy here, and the city has an interesting history. I'm a receptionist in an office in downtown Seattle. My office is in a nice part of the city. It's near a big park.

My home's not in Seattle. It's in Kenmore. Kenmore is a small town near Seattle with about 20,000 people. It's a nice town with a park, two supermarkets, and a hotel. I'm married to Emily, and we have two children.

Our house is near downtown Kenmore. It's a small house, and it's new. It's not near the park, but it is near one of the supermarkets. I'm very happy here. I have a lot of friends in Kenmore and in Seattle, and my job isn't boring!

c Write about your home. Think about these questions:

- Where's your home?
- Is your home big or small? Is it old or new?
- Is your home in a small town or a city?
- Is your town or city interesting or boring?
- What's near your home?

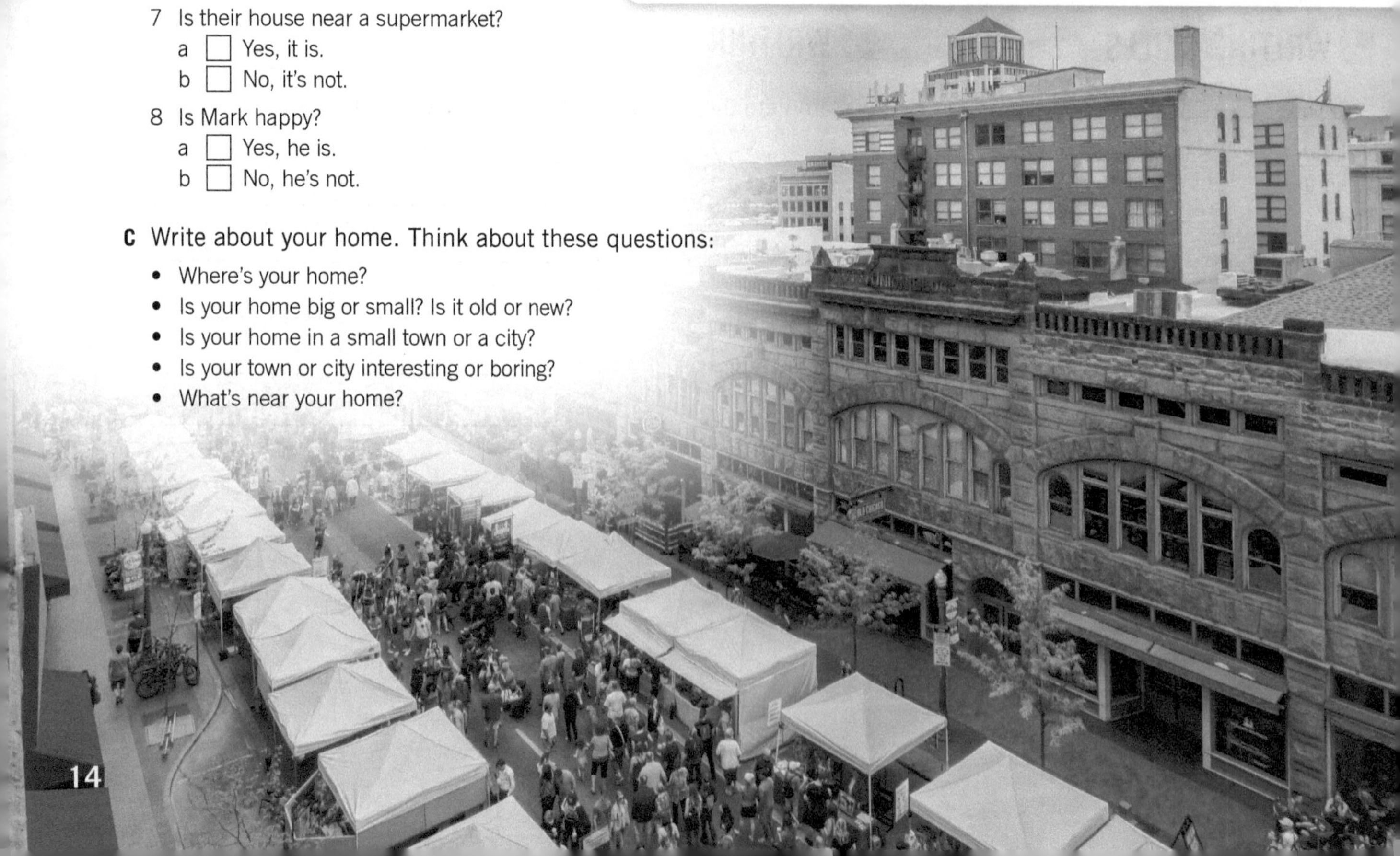

2 LISTENING

a 02.07 Listen. Complete the sentences with the words in the box.

one desk   two desks   three desks

1 Speaker 1, Darren, has ______________.
2 Speaker 2, Paula, has ______________.
3 Speaker 3, Jamie, has ______________.

b 02.07 Listen again. Match pictures a–c to speakers 1–3.

1 ☐ Darren   2 ☐ Paula   3 ☐ Jamie

a

b

c

c 02.07 Listen again. What does each person have on his or her desk? Complete the chart with the words in the box.

apple   glass of water   keys   bag   knife
laptop   newspaper   ~~phone~~   umbrella

Darren	Paula	Jamie
phone		

d Write about your desk. Use the Audioscript on p. 76 to help you. Think about these questions:

- Where is your desk?
- Is your desk old or new?
- Is your desk big or small?
- What is on your desk?
- What isn't on your desk?

Review

1 GRAMMAR

Correct the mistakes.

1 Is this you computer?
   Is this your computer?
2 I have three watch.
3 They're a beautiful town.
4 Beijing is a big cities.
5 This is Kira and Paul, and this is they're house.
6 My apartment is in an old part of town. They're very small.
7 Where's Anna? This is she's bag.
8 Where are the knifes?

2 VOCABULARY

Correct the spelling.

1 eigt tickets
   eight tickets
2 smal bottles of water
3 thirten apartments
4 an intresting city
5 twelv phones
6 beatiful houses
7 an old umbrela
8 funy books

REVIEW YOUR PROGRESS

Look again at Review Your Progress on p. 22 of the Student's Book. How well can you do these things now?
3 = very well   2 = well   1 = not so well

I CAN ...	
talk about my hometown	☐
talk about possessions and common objects	☐
ask for and give personal information.	☐

3A DO YOU LIKE FISH?

1 GRAMMAR Simple present: *I / you / we / they*

a Underline the correct words.

1 We *fruit eat* / *eat fruit* every day.
2 *Do you eat* / *You eat* bread?
3 They *no eat* / *don't eat* eggs.
4 **A** Do you like vegetables?
B No, *don't* / *I don't*.
5 *Like you* / *Do you like* fish?
6 **A** Do you like meat?
B No, we *don't like* / *don't*.
7 I *don't like* / *not like* rice.
8 **A** Do you like fruit?
B Yes, I *do* / *like*.

b 03.01 Listen and check.

c Complete the conversation with the words in the box.

do like don't you eat do you ~~like meat~~ don't eat

DUNCAN Mmm! I [1] like meat ! I eat meat every day!
RAJIT Really? I [2]________ meat.
DUNCAN Oh, you don't eat meat. Do [3]________ fish?
RAJIT No, I [4]________.
DUNCAN [5]________ eat eggs?
RAJIT Yes, I [6]________. I [7]________ eggs.

d 03.02 Listen and check.

2 VOCABULARY Food 1

a Write the words under the pictures.

meat vegetables ~~fish~~ milk tea soda
bread rice coffee juice eggs fruit

 1 fish
 2 ________
 3 ________
 4 ________
 5 ________
 6 ________
 7 ________
 8 ________
 9 ________
 10 ________
 11 ________
 12 ________

b Complete the crossword puzzle.

→ Across
3 M________ is food from animals.
5 E________ are food from chickens.
6 C________ is a drink. It's from Brazil, Colombia, and other countries.
8 R________ is food. It's from China, India, and other countries.
10 A lot of people eat b________ every day.
11 W________ is a drink. It's good for you.

↓ Down
1 Juice is a drink.
2 V________ are food. They're good for you.
4 A lot of people drink t________ every day.
7 F________ is food. It's an animal in the sea.
9 S________ is a drink. It isn't very good for you!

3 PRONUNCIATION Sound and spelling: /i/, /ɪ/, and /aɪ/

a 03.03 Listen to the words in the box. What sound do the letters in **bold** have? Complete the chart.

~~m**y**~~ t**ea** th**i**s r**i**ce m**i**lk **i**s
I w**e** l**i**ke **I**taly m**ea**t k**ey**

/i/ (e.g., *be*)	/ɪ/ (e.g., *it*)	/aɪ/ (e.g., *by*)
		my

3B I USUALLY HAVE DINNER EARLY

1 GRAMMAR Adverbs of frequency

a Underline the correct words.

1 We <u>*sometimes have*</u> / *have sometimes* eggs for breakfast.
2 I *eat never* / *never eat* cookies at work.
3 You *have usually* / *usually have* a sandwich for lunch.
4 They *have always* / *always have* cake on the weekend.
5 I *sometimes eat* / *eat sometimes* an apple at lunchtime.
6 I *have never* / *never have* dinner at 7:00.

b Look at the chart and complete the sentences. Use *always*, *usually*, *sometimes*, or *never* and the simple present of the verbs in parentheses.

1 I __never eat__ fish. (eat)
2 I ________ lunch in a café. (eat)
3 I ________ rice for lunch. (eat)
4 I ________ lunch at work. (have)
5 I ________ cereal for breakfast. (have)
6 I ________ dinner at home. (have)

Food and me	
eat fish	x
eat lunch in a café	every day
eat rice for lunch	on Wednesdays and Saturdays
have lunch at work	x
have cereal for breakfast	on Mondays, Tuesdays, Wednesdays, Thursdays, and Fridays
have dinner at home	every day

2 VOCABULARY Food 2

a Underline the correct words to complete the conversations.

1 **A** What fruit do you like?
B Apples and *sandwiches* / *potatoes* / <u>*bananas*</u>.
2 **A** Would you like *a cookie* / *butter* / *a pizza* with your coffee?
B No thanks.
3 **A** A *sandwich* / *pizza* / *tomato* is a vegetable.
B No, it's not. It's a fruit!
4 **A** We have bread, butter, and eggs.
B Good! *An egg sandwich* / *A cake* / *An apple* for me, please.
5 **A** A cheese *apple* / *pizza* / *ice cream*, please.
B Certainly.
6 **A** Is this fruit juice?
B Yes, it's *cake* / *orange* / *cheese* juice.

b 03.04 Listen and check.

3 VOCABULARY Time

a Look at the clocks and complete the times. Use the words in the box.

after eleven ~~o'clock~~ one quarter (x2) thirty to

1 eight __o'clock__

5 ten ________

2 quarter ________ seven

6 ________ to one

3 ________ o'clock

7 quarter ________ six

4 ________ after one

8 ________ thirty

b 03.05 Listen and check.

4 PRONUNCIATION Sound and spelling: /æ/ and /ɔ/

a 03.06 Listen to the words in the box. What sound do the letters in **bold** have? Complete the chart.

~~m**o**rning~~ **a**fternoon h**a**lf **a**fter f**ou**r cl**a**ss ban**a**na st**o**re

/æ/ (e.g., *gas*)	/ɔ/ (e.g., *your*)
	morning

3C EVERYDAY ENGLISH
I'd like a large coffee, please

1 USEFUL LANGUAGE
Ordering and paying in a café

a Complete the expressions with the words in the box.

water pizza ~~coffee~~ go course cake

1 a large *coffee*
2 a piece of ______
3 here you ______
4 a bottle of ______
5 a slice of ______
6 of ______

b Complete the conversation with the sentences in the box.

No, thanks.
Can I have a large coffee?
OK. Thank you very much.
~~Hello. I'd like a piece of banana bread, please.~~

SERVER Good morning.
NAOMI 1 *Hello. I'd like a piece of banana bread, please.*
SERVER Sure. And to drink?
NAOMI 2 ______
SERVER Of course. With milk?
NAOMI 3 ______
SERVER Here you go. That's $6.50, please.
NAOMI 4 ______
SERVER Thank you.

c 03.07 Listen and check.

d Underline the correct words to complete the conversation.

SERVER Good afternoon.
COLBY Hello. 1 *I have / **I'd like*** a tea, please.
SERVER Sure. And to 2 *eat / drink*?
COLBY 3 *I'd like / I like* a cheese sandwich.
SERVER With tomato?
COLBY No, thanks. And 4 *I'd / can I* have some chocolate cake and a bottle 5 *water / of water*, too?
SERVER Of course! That's $11, please.
COLBY OK. Here 6 *you go / go you.*
SERVER Thank you.

e 03.08 Listen and check.

2 PRONUNCIATION
Stressed and unstressed words

a 03.09 Listen to the phrases. Which words are stressed? Check (✓) the correct box.

1 a [ ] a **slice** **of** pizza
b [✓] a **slice** of **pizza**
2 a [ ] **a** large coffee
b [ ] a **large** **coffee**
3 a [ ] a **bottle** of **water**
b [ ] **a** **bottle** of water
4 a [ ] **a** slice of **cheese**
b [ ] a **slice** of **cheese**
5 a [ ] a **small** **orange** juice
b [ ] **a** small orange **juice**
6 a [ ] a **large** **tea**
b [ ] **a** large **tea**
7 a [ ] a glass **of** **milk**
b [ ] a **glass** of **milk**
8 a [ ] a **piece** of **chocolate** **cake**
b [ ] a piece **of** chocolate **cake**

3C SKILLS FOR WRITING

I'm at a café

1 READING

a Read the text messages. Are the sentences true or false?

1 Tony's with a friend from Spain.
2 Javier's funny.
3 Evie's at work.
4 Felipe and Evie are students.
5 Omar likes his work.
6 Renata's at work.

Tony: Hi, Lisa. I'm at a café with Javier. He's my new friend. He's Spanish. He's very funny. Talk soon!

Evie: Hi, Misha. I'm in a restaurant with Felipe. He's a student in my class. We like our new teacher a lot. She's from Colombia. See you later!

Omar: Hi, Renata. I'm at work. It's boring! Where are you? Why aren't you here?

2 WRITING SKILLS Contractions

a Write the full form of the contractions.

1 I'm ___I am___
2 She's not ______
3 He's ______
4 We don't ______
5 They're not ______
6 It's ______

b Complete the text messages with the words in parentheses. Use contractions.

1 Hi, Emre. ___I'm___ (I am) in a café with Julio and Marta. ______ (They are) really nice! See you later!
2 Hi, Frida. ______ (We are) at the restaurant. ______ (You are not) here! Where are you?
3 Hi, Danny. I ______ (do not) like work! It's boring.
4 Hi, Mel. ______ (We are) in Rome. ______ (It is) a beautiful city! Talk later!
5 Hi, Greg. ______ (I am) at work with Yuri. ______ (He is not) very happy.
6 Hi, Matt. ______ (I am not) happy today. My teacher is boring.

3 WRITING

a Write a text message to a friend. Think about these questions:

- Where are you?
- Are you at work?
- Who are you with?

UNIT 3
Reading and listening extension

1 READING

a Read about meals in Italy. Underline the correct words to complete the sentences.

1 In Italy, people *eat* / *don't eat* a lot of fruit and vegetables.
2 Italians drink a lot of *tea* / *coffee*.
3 They *like* / *don't like* meat and fish.
4 They usually have *three* / *four* meals every day.
5 Italian people *have* / *don't have* pasta every day.
6 For a lot of people, the big meal of the day is in the *afternoon* / *evening*.

b Read the text again. Are the sentences true or false?

1 Breakfast is at 9:00.
2 Maria and her family have coffee and cereal for breakfast.
3 On work days, Maria and her friends have lunch in the office.
4 On weekends, Maria has lunch with her family.
5 A *panino* is a pizza.
6 Dinner is at 8:30.
7 They sometimes have pasta for dinner.
8 They often have cake in the morning.

c Write about the meals you have every day. Think about these questions:

- How many meals do you have?
- What time do you have your meals?
- What do you usually have for breakfast, lunch, and dinner?

MEALS IN ITALY

My name is Maria, and I'm Italian. In Italy, people eat different foods. We like pasta and pizza, but we don't eat them every day. We like a lot of different meat and fish. And we eat a lot of fruit and vegetables.

In my family, we have three meals a day. Breakfast is at eight o'clock. We eat *fette biscottate*, a type of breakfast bread, and have coffee with milk. Italian people usually drink a lot of coffee!

On work days, my lunch is always at one o'clock. I never have lunch in my office. I usually have a *panino* (that's a sandwich) or a slice of pizza with my friends in a café near the office. On the weekend, I have lunch at home with my family.

Dinner is the big meal of the day for a lot of Italians. In my family, we always have dinner at eight thirty. We have rice or pasta, then fish with vegetables. We don't eat a lot of meat. After dinner, we usually have fruit and coffee, but on the weekend we sometimes have cake.

2 LISTENING

a 03.10 Listen to the conversation. Check (✓) the food and drink words you hear.

cheese	✓	banana	☐
meat	☐	ice cream	☐
egg	☐	tea	☐
fish	☐	fruit juice	☐
chocolate	☐	water	☐

b 03.10 Listen again. Check (✓) who says the sentences.

	John	Anna
1 I never eat cheese.	✓	
2 Do you like eggs?		
3 I like eggs.		
4 I eat a lot of tomatoes.		
5 I don't eat a lot of chocolate.		
6 I usually drink tea.		
7 I don't like hot drinks.		
8 I always have orange juice for breakfast.		

c Write about food and drinks you like and don't like. Use these expressions:

- I eat a lot of …
- I don't drink a lot of …
- I never eat …
- I always drink …

Review

1 GRAMMAR

Check (✓) the sentences that are correct. Correct the mistakes.

1 ✓ Do you like eggs?
2 ☐ I never eat cake.
3 ☐ We have sometimes pizza.
4 ☐ They don't like ice cream.
5 ☐ I like fruit.
6 ☐ I not like cheese.
7 ☐ You like meat?
8 ☐ They eat usually pizza for lunch.

2 VOCABULARY

Check (✓) the sentences that are correct. Correct the mistakes.

1 ☐ I like vegtables.
I like vegetables.
2 ☐ We have lunch at 12:45 p.m.
3 ☐ We eat rise for lunch every day.
4 ☐ Do you have an apple?
5 ☐ I never eat cookis.
6 ☐ We have a breakfast at 7:30 a.m.
7 ☐ I don't like cake.
8 ☐ That sanwich is really big!

REVIEW YOUR PROGRESS

Look again at Review Your Progress on p. 30 of the Student's Book. How well can you do these things now?
3 = very well 2 = well 1 = not so well

I CAN …	
say what I eat and drink	☐
talk about food and meals	☐
order and pay in a café.	☐

4A WHAT DO YOU STUDY?

1 GRAMMAR
Simple present: *Wh-* questions

a Put the words in the correct order to make questions.

1 live / where / do / you ?
Where do you live?
2 's / apartment / your / where ?
____
3 lunch / eat / what / for / you / do ?
____
4 are / names / their / what ?
____
5 do / study / where / you ?
____
6 start / when / she / work / does ?
____

b <u>Underline</u> the correct words.

1 What time *is / are / <u>do</u>* you go to the gym?
2 What languages *is / are / do* you speak?
3 What *is / are / do* the time?
4 When *is / are / do* you meet your friends?
5 Where *is / are / do* you from?
6 Where *is / are / do* the university?
7 When *is / are / do* you at home?
8 What *is / are / do* you study?

2 VOCABULARY Common verbs

a Check (✓) the correct words to complete the sentences.

1 You ________ Spanish.
a ☐ live b ☑ speak c ☐ meet
2 We ________ Japanese.
a ☐ meet b ☐ study c ☐ work
3 I ________ my friends every day.
a ☐ meet b ☐ go c ☐ work
4 We ________ soccer.
a ☐ go b ☐ play c ☐ speak
5 I ________ at an English language school.
a ☐ go b ☐ live c ☐ teach
6 We ________ to the gym every day.
a ☐ go b ☐ study c ☐ teach

b Complete the crossword puzzle.

→ Across
2 They ________ to school every day.
4 I ________ English, German, and Portuguese.
5 I ________ young children in a small school.
6 We ________ tennis every day.

↓ Down
1 I work in a factory.
3 I ________ my friends after school.
4 We ________ English at a language school.
7 You ________ in a big house.

3 PRONUNCIATION Stressed words

a 04.01 Listen to the sentences and <u>underline</u> the stressed words.

1 <u>Where</u> do you <u>live</u>?
2 Do you speak French?
3 Do you work in a factory?
4 What do you study?
5 Do you go to the gym?
6 When do you have lunch?

4B SHE HAS A SISTER AND A BROTHER

1 GRAMMAR
Simple present: *he / she / it* affirmative

a Underline the correct words.

1 Pablo *haves* / *<u>has</u>* an international family.
2 My dad *teachs* / *teaches* at the university.
3 Julie *lives* / *livs* in a big house.
4 Sandro *works* / *workes* in an office.
5 My brother *studys* / *studies* math.
6 Camila *plays* / *playes* the guitar.
7 Ryan *speakes* / *speaks* Chinese.
8 My mom *goes* / *gos* to the gym every day.

b Complete the sentences with the correct form of the verbs in parentheses.

1 Dean likes tennis and soccer. (like)
2 My sister ______ to the movies every weekend. (go)
3 Jack ______ Italian at school. (study)
4 Mandy ______ a sister and two brothers. (have)
5 My brother ______ soda every day. (drink)
6 My mom ______ young children. (teach)
7 Enrique ______ at home. (work)
8 My friend Sonya ______ in Berlin. (live)

2 VOCABULARY Numbers 2

a Write the numbers in words.

51 fifty-one
27 ______
45 ______
89 ______
34 ______
98 ______
66 ______
100 ______
72 ______

3 VOCABULARY Family and people

a Look at the family tree. Complete the sentences with the words in the box.

brother	daughter	father	~~husband~~	mother	parents	sister	son	wife

1 Michael is Jane's husband.
2 Michael is Natalie's ______.
3 Jane is Oliver's ______.
4 Ron and Mary are Laura's ______.
5 Oliver is Natalie's ______.
6 Diana is Ron's ______.
7 Oliver is Michael's ______.
8 Natalie is James's ______.
9 Laura is Diana's ______.

4 PRONUNCIATION
Sound and spelling: /ð/

a 04.02 Listen and check (✓) the words that have the /ð/ sound.

1 she ☐
2 that ☐
3 right ☐
4 father ☐
5 mother ☐
6 three ☐
7 they ☐
8 the ☐
9 eight ☐
10 brother ☐

4C EVERYDAY ENGLISH

This is my father

1 USEFUL LANGUAGE

Asking and talking about photos

a Underline the correct words to complete the conversation.

KATIE [1]*Can I see / Do you have* photos of your home?
AMY Yes, [2]*I do / do.*
KATIE [3]*Can I see / This is* them?
AMY Sure. [4]*This is / This* my apartment.
KATIE [5]*Who does / Who's* this?
AMY My brother Harry.
KATIE [6]*Great / Is great* photo!
AMY Thanks. Here's another picture of my apartment.
KATIE [7]*It / It's* really nice.

b 04.03 Listen and check.

c Put the conversation in the correct order.

- [ ] **JENNY** Nice picture! They look like you!
- [1] **JENNY** Do you have photos of your family?
- [ ] **JENNY** Can I see them?
- [ ] **HUGO** Sure. This is my dad and my brother. And this is me with my mom and my sister.
- [ ] **HUGO** Yes, I do.

d 04.04 Listen and check.

2 PRONUNCIATION

Sound and spelling: /tʃ/ and /dʒ/

a 04.05 Listen to the words in the box. What sound do the letters in **bold** have? Complete the chart.

~~oran**ge**~~ ques**t**ion **ch**eap pa**g**e **ch**ild **J**apan **G**ermany mana**g**er pic**t**ure wa**tch**

/tʃ/ (e.g., *lun**ch***)	/dʒ/ (e.g., *chan**ge***)
	orange

SKILLS FOR WRITING
They're a happy family

This is my brother Lucio and his beautiful son Joel. Joel is six years old. They're at home in this picture. They live in a big house in Milan, in Italy. It's a very nice house. Lucio works with computers. He has an office in Porta Nuova.

His wife isn't in the photo. Her name's Vanessa. She's Brazilian. She teaches at the university in Milan. She's very funny. They're a happy family!

1 READING

a Read about the photo. Underline the correct answers.

1 Joel is *six* / *thirty-six*.
2 Lucio and Joel have a *small* / *big* home.
3 They live in *Italy* / *Brazil*.
4 Lucio works with *children* / *computers*.
5 Lucio *is* / *isn't* married.
6 Vanessa is a university *teacher* / *student*.
7 She *lives in* / *is from* Brazil.
8 Vanessa, Lucio, and Joel *are* / *aren't* happy.

2 WRITING SKILLS Word order

a Check (✓) the correct sentences.

1 a ☑ We don't work.
  b ☐ We work don't.
2 a ☐ We eat a big breakfast at home.
  b ☐ We eat at home a big breakfast.
3 a ☐ They don't have a pencil in their bag.
  b ☐ They don't have in their bag a pencil.
4 a ☐ We play at school baseball.
  b ☐ We play baseball at school.
5 a ☐ I like in my coffee sugar.
  b ☐ I like sugar in my coffee.
6 a ☐ She doesn't in London work.
  b ☐ She doesn't work in London.

b Put the words in the correct order to make sentences.

1 his daughters / this / is / my friend / with .
This is my friend with his daughters.
2 Ecuador / live / they / in .
___
3 here / I / live / don't .
___
4 Ruben and Cara / these / children / are / my .
___
5 a / Mexico / have / apartment / small / I / City / in .
___
6 English / at / sister / my / college / studies .
___

3 WRITING

a Write a caption for a favorite photo of you with your friends or family. Give information about:

- who the people are
- where they are
- their jobs or studies.

___
___
___
___

UNIT 4
Reading and listening extension

1 READING

a Read the email and match the people 1–6 to the places a–f.

1	e Daniel	a	Warsaw
2	☐ Marisol	b	Kyoto
3	☐ Elizabetta	c	Guatemala
4	☐ Greg and Claire	d	San Francisco
5	☐ Jon	e	Mexico City
6	☐ Tom	f	Washington

b Read the email again. Complete the family tree with the names in the box.

Jeff Keiko Rei ~~Elizabetta~~
Claire Daniel Greg Tom

Hi Marisol,

Thanks for your email. I love the photos of your family. You have a big family! My family is small. Here's a photo of us on vacation.

I'm with my husband, Greg, our daughter, Linda, and our son, Jeff. My parents, Tom and Elizabetta, are in the photo, too. My dad is American. He's from San Francisco, but my mother comes from Warsaw in Poland. Greg and I live in Washington with our children. Greg works in an office, and I'm a teacher (as you know). Greg's parents live in Washington, too, so we see them one or two days a week, but my mom and dad are in California. We usually see them during the summer.

I have two brothers, Daniel and Jon. They're not in the photo. Daniel is an English teacher in Mexico City, and Jon lives in Kyoto, in Japan. Jon's wife, Keiko, is Japanese, and they have a daughter. Her name's Rei. We sometimes see them during the summer. Rei is five, and she speaks Japanese and English very well.

Write soon and tell me more about your life in Guatemala.

Claire

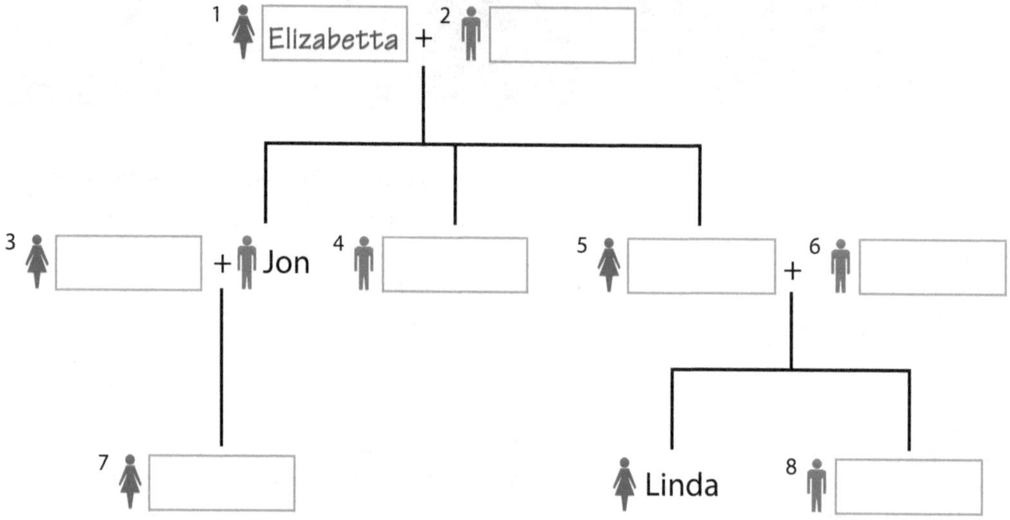

c Draw your family tree and write about the people in your family. Write about:

- their names and ages
- their jobs or studies
- where they live.

2 LISTENING

a 04.06 Listen to the conversation. Put the subjects in the order you hear them.

☐ a vacation
☐ language lessons
☐ working at a university
☐ parents
1 studying at a university

b 04.06 Listen again and underline the correct words.

1 *Philip* / *Kerry* has a job.
2 *Philip* / *Kerry* lives in Boston.
3 *Philip* / *Kerry* studies at a university.
4 *Philip* / *Kerry* works in Hong Kong.
5 *Philip* / *Kerry* lives in a house.
6 *Philip* / *Kerry* has language classes.
7 *Philip* / *Kerry* is on vacation.
8 *Philip's* / *Kerry's* parents live in France.

c Complete the conversation with your own ideas.

A Hi, ____________!
B Hello, ________. How are you?
A I'm fine, thanks. I'm a student at ____________ now.
B Really? What subject do you ____________?
A ____________. Where do you ____________ now?
B I live in ____________ and I work in ____________.
A That's good.
B How ____________ your parents?
A They're fine. They live in ____________ now.
B Really? That's great.

Review

1 GRAMMAR

Correct the mistakes.

1 Where you work?
Where do you work?
2 He work in the Bahamas.
3 She haves two brothers.
4 What your name is?
5 Her husband gos to work in the evening.
6 My sister studys German.
7 Where live you?
8 Where you from?

2 VOCABULARY

Check (✓) the sentences that are correct. Correct the mistakes.

1 ✓ I teach children.
2 ☐ Our English class has six woman and two men.
3 ☐ I speak Turkish.
4 ☐ My sister is twenty and five years old.
5 ☐ I work in Boston.
6 ☐ Their son is thirty-three and their daugter is thirty-five.
7 ☐ His mother is hundred years old.
8 ☐ I meet interesting peoples at work.

REVIEW YOUR PROGRESS

Look again at Review Your Progress on p. 38 of the Student's Book. How well can you do these things now?
3 = very well   2 = well   1 = not so well

I CAN ...	
talk about my life and ask about others	☐
talk about my family	☐
ask and talk about photos.	☐

5A THERE ARE A FEW STORES

1 GRAMMAR *there is / there are*: affirmative

a Put the words in the correct order to make sentences.

1 here / there / 's / school / one .
There's one school here.
2 teachers / two / there / are .
______
3 cars / are / few / a / there .
______
4 a / there / 's / small / museum .
______
5 are / families / ten / there .
______
6 there / old / an / 's / hospital .
______

b 05.01 Listen and check.

c Complete the sentences with *there's* or *there are*.

1 *There are* a lot of people.
2 ______ a good café near the hotel.
3 ______ an interesting store on this street.
4 ______ about 50 families.
5 ______ a few new houses and apartments.
6 ______ a very small school.
7 ______ 72 big houses.
8 ______ one bank.

2 PRONUNCIATION Sound and spelling: /uː/ and /ʌ/

a 05.02 Listen to the words in the box. What sound do the letters in **bold** have? Complete the chart.

~~f**ew**~~ b**u**tter s**o**metimes s**u**permarket sch**oo**l st**u**dy b**eau**tiful p**oo**l l**o**ve wh**o** f**u**nny m**o**ther

/uː/ (e.g., *you*)	/ʌ/ (e.g., *cup*)
few	

3 VOCABULARY Places in a town

a Write the words under the pictures.

park hospital ~~store~~ hotel beach café movie theater school bank bus stop restaurant swimming pool

1 *store*

2 ______

3 ______

4 ______

5 ______

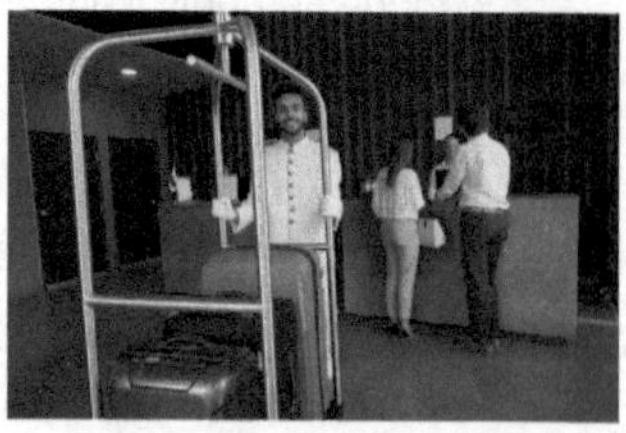
6 ______

7 ______

8 ______

9 ______

10 ______

11 ______

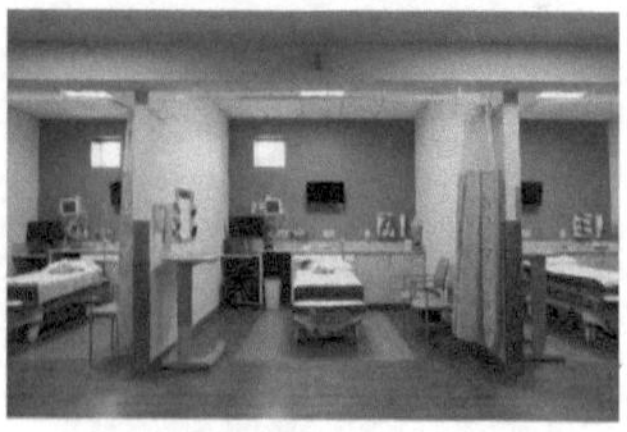
12 ______

5B IS THERE A HOSTEL IN YOUR TOWN?

1 GRAMMAR *there is / there are*: negative and questions

a Check (✓) the correct words to complete the sentences.

1 There isn't ______________ in the room.
a ☑ a TV   b ☐ two TVs

2 Are there any good ______________ in this town?
a ☐ restaurant   b ☐ restaurants

3 There aren't ______________ on the first floor.
a ☐ a big room   b ☐ any big rooms

4 There aren't any ______________ here.
a ☐ store   b ☐ stores

5 Is there ______________ near here?
a ☐ a café   b ☐ any cafés

6 Is there ______________ near the station?
a ☐ a bank   b ☐ banks

b Underline the correct words to complete the conversations.

Conversation 1

A [1]*There is* / *<u>Is there</u>* a bathtub in the room?

B No, there [2]*isn't* / *aren't*. But there [3]*are* / *is* a shower.

Conversation 2

A There [4]*aren't any* / *isn't a* hotels in this town.

B Oh.

A [5]*There aren't any* / *There's a* hostel on Maple Street. It's really good.

B OK. Thanks.

Conversation 3

B [6]*Is there* / *There is* parking at this hotel?

A Yes, there is. And it's free.

B [7]*Are there any* / *Is there an* empty rooms on the first floor?

A No, there [8]*aren't* / *isn't*. Sorry. But there [9]*are* / *isn't* a lot of empty rooms on the top floor.

B Oh. No thanks.

c 05.03 Listen and check.

2 PRONUNCIATION Sound and spelling: /ʃ/

a 05.04 Listen and check (✓) the words that have the /ʃ/ sound.

1 ☐ bath
2 ☐ shower
3 ☐ China
4 ☐ Russia
5 ☐ she
6 ☐ sure
7 ☐ six
8 ☐ finish
9 ☐ museum
10 ☐ shop
11 ☐ station
12 ☐ movies

3 VOCABULARY Hotels

a Complete the sentences. Use the letters in parentheses.

1 There's a big bathtub, but there isn't any hot water. (b h u t a t b)
2 It's very cold. Can I have a ______________ for my bed, please? (n e k l a b t)
3 There's free ______________ here, but I don't have my computer with me. (f i i w)
4 The ______________'s very good, and there's a lot of hot water. (o r w s h e)
5 There's a big ______________ for meetings on the second floor. (o m o r)
6 Can I have a ______________, please? I want to use the swimming pool. (o w e l t)
7 There's free ______________ at this hotel. You can leave your car here. (n p g a i r k)
8 There's one small ______________ on the bed. (w o l p l i)

b Complete the crossword puzzle.

→ Across

1 I often sit in a bathtub of hot water to relax.
3 There are a lot of cars in the ______________ lot.
4 **A** Jason's at the swimming pool.
B Does he have a ______________?
A Oh no! It's on his bed.
6 **A** Can I take a ______________?
B You can, but there isn't any hot water.

↓ Down

1 **A** I'm cold.
B Use the ______________ that's on the bed.
2 Do you like watching movies on ______________ or at the movie theater?
3 **A** There are three big ______________ on my bed.
B Are they soft?
5 **A** There isn't any ______________.
B Oh, that's OK. I don't need to use the Internet.
7 We need two ______________ at the hotel. One for my parents and one for my brother and me.

5C EVERYDAY ENGLISH

Is there a café near here?

1 USEFUL LANGUAGE
Asking and saying where places are

a Complete the sentences and questions with the words in the box.

it's near ~~where's~~ there there's

1 Where's the hospital?
2 Is ______ a park near here?
3 Are there any restaurants ______ here?
4 ______ one on this street.
5 ______ on the next street.

b Complete the conversation with the sentences in the box.

OK. And is there a museum near here?
Oh yes! Great! Thanks for your help.
~~Excuse me, can you help me?~~
Is there a movie theater near here?

A 1 Excuse me, can you help me?
B Yes, of course.
A 2 ______
B No, I'm sorry. There aren't any movie theaters near here. But there are two downtown.
A 3 ______
B Yes, there is. It's on this street. Just over there.
A 4 ______
B No problem.

c 05.05 Listen and check.

d Complete the conversation with the words in the box.

any ~~can~~ course for next near no sorry

A Excuse me, 1 can you help me?
B Yes, of 2 ______.
A Are there any hotels 3 ______ here?
B Yes, there are. There's one on the 4 ______ street.
A Oh, good. And are there 5 ______ hostels – cheap hostels?
B No, I'm 6 ______. There aren't.
A OK. Thanks 7 ______ your help.
B 8 ______ problem.

e 05.06 Listen and check.

2 PRONUNCIATION
Emphasizing what you say 1

a 05.07 Listen to the sentences. Which words are stressed? Check (✓) the correct box.

1 a ☐ It's a very good hotel.
  b ☑ It's a very good hotel.
2 a ☐ It's so hot today!
  b ☐ It's so hot today!
3 a ☐ I'm really sorry.
  b ☐ I'm really sorry.
4 a ☐ This room's really nice.
  b ☐ This room's really nice.
5 a ☐ It's a very big school.
  b ☐ It's a very big school.
6 a ☐ This TV is so old!
  b ☐ This TV is so old!
7 a ☐ The museum's really boring.
  b ☐ The museum's really boring.
8 a ☐ The bathroom's very small.
  b ☐ The bathroom's very small.

5C SKILLS FOR WRITING
It's not cheap, but it's nice

1 READING

a Read the email. Are the sentences true or false?

1 The hotel is near the station.
2 Monica and Kalina don't like the hotel.
3 Monica and Kalina like the things in their room.
4 The hotel is expensive.
5 The hotel has a lot of available rooms.
6 Monica and Kalina like the hotel manager.
7 There's a restaurant in the hotel.
8 Monica and Kalina play the guitar in the evening.

Hi Lexi,

We're at the Station Hotel. It's not a big new hotel near the station. It's an old station near the beach! It's great! The rooms are small, but they're very good.

Our room is on the first floor. There are beautiful flowers in the room, and there are a lot of pillows and blankets on the beds. It's not cheap, but we're only here for three nights.

There are a lot of people here. There aren't any available rooms! All the people are very friendly, and the manager's nice. In the evenings, we have dinner at the Old Station restaurant. It's in the hotel. The food is good, and an old man plays the guitar.

See you soon,

Monica and Kalina

2 WRITING SKILLS *and* and *but*

a Check (✓) the correct ending for the sentences.

1 I live in Rome, but …
  a ☐ I speak Italian.
  b ☑ I don't speak Italian.
2 The movie theater's big, but …
  a ☐ it's very old.
  b ☐ it's great.
3 The high school is good, and …
  a ☐ he'd like to study there.
  b ☐ he wouldn't like to study there.
4 The café has great coffee, and …
  a ☐ it has free Wi-Fi.
  b ☐ it doesn't have free Wi-Fi.
5 There isn't a bookstore, but …
  a ☐ there is a library.
  b ☐ there isn't a library.
6 My office is nice, and …
  a ☐ it's not near my house.
  b ☐ it's near my house.

b Complete the sentences with *and* or *but*.

1 There's a bathtub, ___and___ there's a shower.
2 The room is small, ______ it's OK.
3 There's a supermarket on the next street, ______ it's not very big.
4 The city is beautiful, ______ it's boring.
5 The hotel has big rooms, ______ they're very beautiful.
6 There's a café on the first floor, ______ there's a gym on the second floor.
7 It's a beautiful hotel, ______ they don't have any available rooms.
8 There's a shower, ______ there isn't any hot water!

3 WRITING

a Imagine that you are at a hotel in a new town. Write an email to a friend. Describe the hotel and the town.

Hi ______,

____

____

____

____

____

____

____

____

____

See you soon,

______

UNIT 5
Reading and listening extension

1 READING

a Read the texts. Check (✓) the things you read about.

1 ☐ a bank
2 ☐ a swimming pool
3 ☐ a movie theater
4 ☐ a hospital
5 ☐ a hotel
6 ☐ a parking lot
7 ☐ a museum
8 ☐ a park
9 ☑ a school
10 ☐ a supermarket

b Read the texts again. <u>Underline</u> the correct words to complete the sentences.

1 *Daria* / *<u>Geraldo</u>* / *Elam* lives near a supermarket.
2 *Daria* / *Geraldo* / *Elam* doesn't have any children.
3 The hospital is on *Holly Road* / *Broadway Avenue* / *Clarkson Road.*
4 *Holly Road* / *Broadway Avenue* / *Clarkson Road* is a good place to see movies.
5 The park is near *Holly Road* / *Broadway Avenue* / *Clarkson Road.*
6 There's a *station* / *museum* / *park* on Broadway Avenue.
7 Daria takes her son to the *swimming pool* / *ice cream shop* / *movie theater* in the summer.
8 There are a lot of *stores* / *cafés* / *offices* near Geraldo's home.

c Write about your street. Think about these questions:

- What is the name of your street?
- Where is your street?
- What is there on or near your street?
- Is it an interesting place to live or work?

MY STREET

I work downtown, but I live on Clarkson Road. Clarkson Road isn't near downtown, but it is a nice place. There are about 60 houses, and there's a school and a store where I buy food every week. There's also a little park near the train station. It has an ice cream shop, and in the summer, I sometimes take my son to the park for ice cream.

1 DARIA

I live on Holly Road with my wife and daughter. It's not a very interesting place to live, but it's easy to get to work because I work at Holly Road Hospital. There are a lot of offices and apartments on my road, but there aren't any stores or restaurants. It isn't a problem. There's a big supermarket near Holly Road, and there are a lot of buses that go downtown.

2 GERALDO

I live and work on Broadway Avenue. It is downtown. There are a lot of different stores and cafés here, and there are two bookstores. I work in the bookstore near the museum. When I'm not at work, I sometimes go to the movie theater. Broadway Avenue is a good place to live. My apartment is on the first floor, and I sometimes sit and watch the people on the street. There is always something interesting to see.

3 ELAM

2 LISTENING

a 05.08 Listen to Yusuf and a receptionist at a tourist office. Are the sentences true or false?

1 It is summer.
2 There are a lot of empty rooms.
3 Yusuf has a lot of money.
4 Yusuf chooses a room at the Star Hostel.

b 05.08 Listen again. Complete the chart with the words in the box.

café cheap friendly expensive free Wi-Fi ~~near the beach~~ small clean rooms rooms with bathtubs TVs in rooms free breakfast near the train station rooms with showers

Hotel Splendor	Star Hostel
near the beach	

c 05.08 Listen again. <u>Underline</u> the correct words.

1 Yusuf wants a room for a *<u>weekend</u>* / *week*.
2 The room is for *one person* / *two people*.
3 He wants to stay near the *train station* / *beach*.
4 Rooms at the Hotel Splendor are *$140* / *$160*.
5 Single rooms at the Star Hostel are *$40* / *$60*.
6 There is a café on the *first* / *second* floor of the Star Hostel.
7 There are *two* / *three* supermarkets near the hostel.
8 *Yusuf* / *The receptionist* wants to call the hostel.

d Complete the conversation with your own ideas.

RECEPTIONIST Good morning. Can I help you?
VISITOR Hi. I'd like a hotel room for ______ nights near the ______.
RECEPTIONIST The Royal Hotel is near there. The rooms have ______ and ______, and it's ______ dollars a night.
VISITOR Hmm... That's very expensive. I don't have a lot of money.
RECEPTIONIST Well, there's the Comfort Hotel on this street. It doesn't have ______, but it's cheap.
VISITOR OK.
RECEPTIONIST Do you want the Comfort Hotel's phone number?
VISITOR Yes, please.

Review

1 GRAMMAR

Check (✓) the sentences that are correct. Correct the mistakes.

1 ☐ There is a park here?
Is there a park here?
2 ☐ There is two movie theaters.
3 ☐ There aren't any supermarkets.
4 ☐ Are there any cafés on this street?
5 ☐ No, there not.
6 ☐ Is there a hotel near here?
7 ☐ Yes, there's.
8 ☐ There not any stores here.

2 VOCABULARY

Correct the spelling.

1 I like this restarant.
I like this restaurant.
2 Where's the scool?
3 Is there a swiming pool?
4 Can I have a blankit, please?
5 There isn't a pilow on the bed.
6 Where's the hospittal?
7 We often go to the beech.
8 Do you have a towl?

REVIEW YOUR PROGRESS

Look again at Review Your Progress on p. 46 of the Student's Book. How well can you do these things now?
3 = very well 2 = well 1 = not so well

I CAN ...	
describe a town	☐
talk about hotels and hostels	☐
ask about and say where places are.	☐

6A I DON'T WORK AT NIGHT

1 GRAMMAR
Simple present: *he / she / it* negative

a Underline the correct words.

1 Shona *don't* / *doesn't* work in an office.
2 I *don't* / *doesn't* work on Wednesdays.
3 Tomás doesn't *meet* / *meets* interesting people at his job.
4 We *don't* / *doesn't* speak a lot at work.
5 Mark *don't* / *doesn't* study Italian. He studies Spanish.
6 Selena doesn't *likes* / *like* her job.
7 You *don't* / *doesn't* live here!
8 He *don't* / *doesn't* eat meat.

b Complete the sentences with the correct form of the verbs in parentheses.

1 Moira doesn't eat cake, cookies, or ice cream. (not / eat)
2 You ________ young children. (not / teach)
3 Anton ________ coffee. (not / like)
4 My brother ________ in this house. (not / live)
5 My parents ________. (not / work)
6 Dana ________ to the movies with her friends. (not / go)
7 I ________ his name. (not / know)
8 The doctor ________ Spanish. (not / speak)

2 VOCABULARY Jobs

a Match the words in the box with the pictures.

chef doctor factory worker soccer player
office worker receptionist sales assistant
student ~~taxi driver~~ server

1 taxi driver

2 ________

3 ________

4 ________

5 ________

6 ________

7 ________

8 ________

9 ________

10 ________

b Underline the correct words.

1 Hello, I'm Natasha. I'm the hotel *assistant* / *receptionist*.
2 **A** What's your brother's job?
  B He's a *businessman* / *businesswoman*.
3 I'm an IT *worker* / *player*. I work with computers.
4 I'm a taxi *worker* / *driver*. I sometimes work at night.
5 I work at this restaurant. I'm a *teacher* / *chef*.
6 Lionel Messi is a soccer *assistant* / *player*.
7 **A** Does your sister work at Bank One?
  B Yes, she's a *bank teller* / *factory worker*.
8 **A** Excuse me! Are you a *doctor* / *driver*?
  B Yes, I am. Can I help you?

c 06.01 Listen and check.

3 PRONUNCIATION
Sound and spelling: /ʃ/ and /tʃ/

a 06.02 Listen to the sentences. Choose the sentence with the same sounds in **bold**.

1 The **ch**ildren are in the kit**ch**en.
  a ☐ The ma**ch**ine accepts ca**sh**.
  b ☑ This **ch**air is **ch**eap.
2 **Sh**e fini**sh**es work late.
  a ☐ Please wa**sh** the di**sh**es.
  b ☐ Na**ch**os have **ch**eese and **ch**ips.
3 I'd like a **ch**icken sandwi**ch**, please.
  a ☐ The recep**t**ionist is at the bus sta**t**ion.
  b ☐ The **ch**ild plays at the bea**ch**.
4 **Ch**eck the **ch**art.
  a ☐ **Sh**e's very spe**c**ial to me.
  b ☐ Our tea**ch**er likes **ch**ocolate cake.
5 The **ch**ef is **sh**ort.
  a ☐ Please **sh**are the informa**t**ion.
  b ☐ He **ch**ooses **ch**icken at the supermarket.

6B I WAKE UP AT 4:00

1 GRAMMAR Simple present: *he / she / it* questions

a Put the words in the correct order to make questions.

1 your / up / husband / early / get / does ?
Does your husband get up early?
2 Eduardo / work / does / where ?
____
3 up / does / what / Richard / wake / time ?
____
4 does / feel / how / Amy / work / after ?
____
5 have / home / at / does / breakfast / Carol ?
____
6 what / work / do / your / sister / does / at ?
____

b Complete the sentences with the words in the box.

do Kathy	does she	does	he does	~~does Lottie live~~	Martin get

1 **A** Where *does Lottie live* ?
B In Germany.
2 **A** __________ your husband work at night?
B No, he doesn't.
3 When does __________ home?
4 Can I call your sister tomorrow morning? What time __________ wake up?
5 When __________ and Jim finish work?
6 **A** Does he study English?
B Yes, __________.

c 06.03 Listen and check.

2 VOCABULARY Daily routine

a Put the daily routine in the correct order.

☐ finish work
☐ get up
☐ go to bed
☐ go to work
☐ have dinner
☐ have lunch
☐ start work
1 wake up

b Complete the sentences with the verbs in the box.

arrive	finish	get	go (x2)	have	start	~~wake~~

1 I *wake* up at 7:00 a.m., and I __________ up at 7:15 a.m.
2 I __________ breakfast at home.
3 I __________ to work every day.
4 I __________ work at 9:00 a.m., and I __________ work at 5:30 p.m.
5 I __________ home at 6:30 p.m.
6 I __________ to bed at 11:00 p.m.

c 06.04 Listen and check.

3 PRONUNCIATION Consonant clusters

a 06.05 Listen and complete the words. Write two letters to make a consonant cluster.

1 *t w* enty
2 _ _ eakfast
3 _ _ anish
4 _ _ ay
5 _ _ uit
6 _ _ ass

6C EVERYDAY ENGLISH

I'll come with you

1 USEFUL LANGUAGE
Making and accepting offers

a Underline the correct words to complete the conversation.

MAX [1]*Do / Would* you like a cup of coffee?
EVA Yes, please.
MAX And [2]*you would / would you* like a piece of cake?
EVA No, [3]*OK / that's OK*, thanks.
MAX Hmm... I need to go to the store. There isn't any coffee here!
EVA I'll [4]*can come / come* with you.
MAX [5]*That / That's* great, thanks. And I need to make the cake... I don't have any!
EVA [6]*I / I'll* help you.
MAX Thank you. [7]*It's / That's* very nice of you.

b 06.06 Listen and check.

c Put the conversation in the correct order.

☐ **UMA** I need to make lunch for José and Karina.
☐ **UMA** And would you like a piece of cake?
☐ **UMA** All right. Thanks. We need pizzas.
☐ **UMA** Don't worry. It's OK. The pizzas at the supermarket are fine.
☐ **UMA** Thank you. That's great.
[1] **UMA** Would you like a cup of coffee, Raul?
☐ **RAUL** No, I'm fine, thanks – just coffee, please.
☐ **RAUL** I'll help you.
☐ **RAUL** I can make pizzas. I make very good pizzas!
☐ **RAUL** Yes, please.
☐ **RAUL** OK, I'll go to the supermarket.

d 06.07 Listen and check.

2 PRONUNCIATION
Emphasizing what you say 2

a 06.08 Listen to the sentences. Which words are stressed? Check (✓) the correct box.

1 **A** I need to make dinner for eight people!
B a ☐ I can help you.
b ☑ I can help you.

2 **A** I need to go to the supermarket, but I'm really busy.
B a ☐ I'll go.
b ☐ I'll go.

3 **A** Oh no! I don't have any money with me!
B a ☐ I can pay.
b ☐ I can pay.

4 **A** I can't open this bottle of water!
B a ☐ I'll do it.
b ☐ I'll do it.

5 **A** I need to go to the store. Can you drive me?
B a ☐ Sorry, but I'm really busy. Jim can take you.
b ☐ Sorry, but I'm really busy. Jim can take you.

6 **A** I need some cups. Do you have any cups?
B a ☐ No, I don't. I can give you some glasses.
b ☐ No, I don't. I can give you some glasses.

6C SKILLS FOR WRITING

She's a taxi driver because she likes driving

1 READING

a Read the email and check (✓) the correct answers.

> Hi Mom,
>
> Life here in New York is exciting!
>
> I have a job at a café in Manhattan. I get up at a quarter to five in the morning every day from Monday to Saturday, and I work from five thirty until two o'clock in the afternoon.
>
> There are a lot of people in the café from six until nine o'clock because the breakfasts here are great! I really like the breakfasts! The sandwiches are also really good, and I have lunch there every day.
>
> I have a new friend in New York. His name's Rex, and he's a taxi driver. He often works at night, and he has breakfast in the café at five thirty. He always says, "Coffee and breakfast for dinner, please!" Then he goes home, and he goes to bed.
>
> Email me soon!
>
> Love,
> Ivan

1 Where does Ivan work?
   a ☐ in a restaurant
   b ☐ in a shop
   c ☑ in a café

2 What time does Ivan get up?
   a ☐ 4:15 a.m.
   b ☐ 4:30 a.m.
   c ☐ 4:45 a.m.

3 Ivan doesn't work on ____________.
   a ☐ Mondays
   b ☐ Saturdays
   c ☐ Sundays

4 What time does Ivan start work?
   a ☐ 5:30 a.m.
   b ☐ 9:00 a.m.
   c ☐ 2:00 p.m.

5 Ivan likes ____________ at the café.
   a ☐ the breakfasts
   b ☐ the sandwiches
   c ☐ the breakfasts and the sandwiches

6 Rex goes to the café at 5:30 a.m. because he ____________.
   a ☐ always starts work at 6:00 a.m.
   b ☐ often finishes work in the morning
   c ☐ works at the café

2 WRITING SKILLS *because* and *also*

a Correct the mistakes.

1 Diana's a taxi driver. Because she likes driving.
   Diana's a taxi driver because she likes driving.
2 They have breakfast at school. They have also lunch at school.
   ____
3 I study business at college. I also am a server.
   ____
4 She gets up early. She goes also to bed early.
   ____
5 He's a teacher because he gets up early.
   ____
6 She sometimes works at night. Because she's a doctor.
   ____

b Complete the sentences with *also* or *because*.

1 There's a museum in my hometown. There's also a movie theater.
2 She speaks Japanese ____________ she's from Japan.
3 I play baseball. I ____________ play tennis.
4 He goes to bed at 8 a.m. ____________ he works at night.
5 My parents have a cat ____________ they love animals.
6 I have black hair. My mom ____________ has black hair.

3 WRITING

a Write an email about the daily routine of one of your friends or a member of your family. Use the email in exercise 1 to help you.

____
____
____
____
____
____
____
____
____

UNIT 6
Reading and listening extension

1 READING

a Read the magazine article. Complete the sentences with the words in the box.

at night	in the afternoon	in the evening
in the morning	on the weekend	

1 Claudia sees her friends ______________.
2 She has classes at the university ______________.
3 She goes to the university library ______________.
4 From Monday to Friday, she goes to work ______________.
5 She works until 11:30 ______________.

b Read the article again. Are the sentences true or false?

1 Claudia studies in her home country.
2 Claudia likes her classes.
3 Her classes start at 8 a.m.
4 She doesn't go home in the afternoon.
5 She has dinner at home.
6 She goes to work after dinner.
7 She finishes work at 11:30.
8 She works all weekend.

c Write a short description of your day. Think about these questions:

- What time do you get up and go to bed?
- What do you do in the morning, afternoon, and evening?
- When do you see your friends?

College *Life*

College is expensive in the U.S., and students also need to pay for textbooks, food, and a place to live. A lot of students work to get extra money. Is it a good idea?

Let's ask a student.

Claudia, 23

I'm a student in New York, but I'm from Colorado. I love my classes, but New York is expensive, so I work in a movie theater in the evenings and on Saturdays.

My day usually starts at 7:45 a.m. when I get up and have breakfast. Then I go to my classes at the university. They start at 9:00 a.m. and finish at 12:30 p.m. There aren't any classes in the afternoon, so I study in the university library. I have something to eat in the student cafeteria, and I walk to the movie theater. My working hours are 6:00 p.m. to 11:30 p.m. from Monday to Friday and 1:30 p.m. to 11:30 p.m. on Saturdays. Sunday is my free day, and I play tennis or go to a museum with my friends.

My job is OK, but I don't want to work six days a week. I get home late, and I only get six or seven hours' sleep. Sometimes, I feel very tired in my classes, and I want to sleep. That isn't good.

2 LISTENING

a 06.09 Listen to the interview. Underline the correct answers.

1 Ian Baker is *American* / *Canadian*.
2 He is a *factory worker* / *businessman*.
3 Ian is *single* / *married*.
4 Ian and Rita have a factory near *Detroit* / *Chicago*.
5 *Eighty* / *Ninety* people work in the factory.
6 Their customers are in *Canada* / *Asia* and South America.

b 06.09 Listen again and underline the correct words.

1 Ian and Rita *have* / *don't have* a computer factory in Michigan.
2 The factory *makes* / *doesn't make* computers for hospitals.
3 Ian *works* / *doesn't work* about 12 hours a day.
4 Ian *sits* / *doesn't sit* in his office every day.
5 Ian *meets* / *doesn't meet* the people who use his computers.
6 Ian and Rita *have* / *don't have* customers in the U.S.
7 Ian *speaks* / *doesn't speak* a foreign language.
8 Rita *goes* / *doesn't go* to South America with Ian.

c Complete the conversation with your own ideas.

INTERVIEWER Welcome to the show. This week, we're talking to people who live and work in ____________. Today, my guest is ____________. Where in ____________ do you live?
GUEST I live in ____________.
INTERVIEWER And what do you do?
GUEST I'm a(n) ____________.
INTERVIEWER That's interesting. Do you like your work?
GUEST ____________ because ____________.
INTERVIEWER Do you work long hours?
GUEST ____________.
INTERVIEWER And do you visit places for work?
GUEST ____________.
INTERVIEWER Thanks very much for talking to us today.

Review

1 GRAMMAR

Correct the mistakes.

1 Lee doesn't works on Mondays.
Lee doesn't work on Mondays.
2 Does he speaks English?
3 When Anna arrives home?
4 Pedro like fish?
5 Seb not plays tennis.
6 **A** Does Becky live here?
B Yes, she lives.
7 **A** Does Russell have a computer?
B No, he not.
8 Where she lives?

2 VOCABULARY

Check (✓) the sentences that are correct. Correct the mistakes.

1 ☑ I wake up at 6:30 a.m.
2 ☐ He gets up at 6:30 a.m.
3 ☐ She's a driver taxi.
4 ☐ I have a lunch at work.
5 ☐ He's a businesman.
6 ☐ She's a chef.
7 ☐ I'm a receptionist.
8 ☐ I go bed at 11:00 p.m.

REVIEW YOUR PROGRESS

Look again at Review Your Progress on p. 54 of the Student's Book. How well can you do these things now?
3 = very well 2 = well 1 = not so well

I CAN ...	
talk about people's jobs	☐
talk about daily routines and habits	☐
make and accept offers.	☐

7A I LIKE THIS LAMP

1 GRAMMAR *this, that, these, those*

a Complete the sentences with the words in the box.

this that these those

1 Do you like ______ flowers?

2 Do you like ______ flowers?

3 I'd like ______ car.

4 I want ______ car!

b 07.01 Listen and check.

c Complete the sentences with *this, that, these,* or *those*. Remember *near* = here (near me) and *far* = there (not near me).

1 ___That___ picture's interesting. (far)
2 ______ plates are nice. (near)
3 I like ______ chair. (near)
4 How much is ______ guitar? (far)
5 I like ______ store. (near)
6 ______ bags are beautiful. (far)
7 I don't like ______ lamp. (far)
8 How much are ______ speakers? (near)

2 VOCABULARY Common objects 2

a Complete the sentences with the words in the box.

book glass ~~clock~~ ball guitar picture plant plate speakers suitcase

1 What time is it? There isn't a ___clock___ in this room.
2 Can I have a ______ for this pizza, please?
3 Would you like a ______ of water?
4 I have lots of clothes, but this bag's very small. I need a big ______.
5 I have a great ______ of my family. Do you want to see it?
6 This is my English ______. It's called *American Empower*.
7 Simon teaches music to children. He often takes his ______ to school for music lessons.
8 My new car stereo has great ______. The sound is really good!
9 What's that ______ in the yard? Its flowers are very nice.
10 We want to play soccer, but we don't have a ______.

3 VOCABULARY Prices

a Check (✓) the correct words.

1 This glass is $10.50.
a ☐ ten dollars and fifty
b ☑ ten dollars and fifty cents
c ☐ one hundred and five dollars

2 This soccer ball is $30.
a ☐ thirty dollar
b ☐ thirteen dollars
c ☐ thirty dollars

3 That guitar is $129.
a ☐ one hundred dollars and twenty-nine
b ☐ one hundred and twenty-nine dollars
c ☐ one hundred and nine-twenty dollars

4 That picture is $24.75.
a ☐ twenty-four dollars and seventy-five cents
b ☐ forty-two dollars and seventy-five cents
c ☐ seventy-five dollars and twenty-four cents

5 Those cups are $9.50.
a ☐ ninety-five dollars and cents
b ☐ nine dollars and fifty cents
c ☐ five dollars and ninety cents

6 These plants are $3.89.
a ☐ three dollars and eighty-nine cents
b ☐ three dollar eighty-nine cent
c ☐ three of dollars eighty-nine cents

b 07.02 Listen and check.

4 PRONUNCIATION Sound and spelling: /b/, /p/, /g/, and /k/

a 07.03 Listen to the words. Write the missing letters.

1 ball
2 suit_ase
3 _lass
4 _a_
5 _late
6 lam_
7 _uitar
8 _oo_
9 _up
10 _lant

7B IT'S OSCAR'S T-SHIRT

1 GRAMMAR
Possessive *'s*; Review of adverbs

a Put the words in the correct order to make sentences. Add an apostrophe (') where needed. There may be more than one possible answer.

1 bag / it's / Kates .
It's Kate's bag.
2 Darrens / they're / shoes .
______
3 brown / friends / jacket / is / my .
______
4 the / are / new / boys / pants .
______
5 I / jeans / never / wear .
______
6 clothes / I / my / sisters / sometimes / wear .
______

b 07.04 Listen and check.

c Complete the sentences with the names and nouns in parentheses and the possessive *'s*.

1 This is Anna's T-shirt. (Anna)
2 Where's ______ phone? (Mehmet)
3 I like ______ new house. (Juan and Laura)
4 That's ______ computer. (the girls)
5 What's ______ phone number? (Sofia)
6 I like ______ shoes. (the children)

2 VOCABULARY Clothes and colors

a Complete the sentences with the words in the box.

black blue brown green ~~gray~~ red white yellow

1 Older people often have gray hair.
2 Chocolate is usually ______.
3 Bananas are ______.
4 Milk is ______.
5 Strawberries are ______.
6 Grass is ______.
7 A tiger is orange and ______.
8 On a sunny day, the sky is ______.

b Complete the crossword puzzle.

↓ Down
1 I bought this jacket to wear with my green dress.
2 It's comfortable to wear a ______ and jeans.
4 Tom Ford is a ______ designer.
8 Don't buy ______ that are too big. They're difficult to walk in!

→ Across
3 You wear ______ on your legs.
5 Light is the opposite of ______.
6 black + white = ______
7 Some women wear a ______ to work.
9 red + ______ = pink

3 PRONUNCIATION
Sound and spelling: /ʃ/ and /dʒ/

a 07.05 Listen to the words in the box. What sound do the letters in **bold** have? Complete the chart.

~~**j**eans~~ lar**g**e fa**sh**ion **sh**oes na**t**ionality **J**apanese vege**t**ables **sh**irt **G**ermany **s**ure **g**ym **sh**op

/ʃ/ (e.g., ***sh**e*)	/dʒ/ (e.g., *chan**g**e*)
	jeans

7C EVERYDAY ENGLISH
Can I help you?

1 USEFUL LANGUAGE Going shopping

a Complete the conversations with the sentences in the box.

Here's your receipt.
No, thanks. Can I look around?
~~Enter your PIN, please.~~
I'd like that T-shirt, please.
How much are these bags?

1 **A** That's $52.95, please.
B Can I pay with a card?
A Sure. Enter your PIN, please.
2 **A** Can I help you?
B ____________________
A Of course.
3 **A** ____________________
B Thanks.
4 **A** ____________________
B They're $35 each.
5 **A** ____________________
B Sure. Here you go.

b 07.06 Listen and check.

c Put the conversation in the correct order.

☐ **SALES ASSISTANT** Thank you.
1 **SALES ASSISTANT** Hi! Can I help you?
☐ **SALES ASSISTANT** Sure. That's $16, please.
☐ **SALES ASSISTANT** They're $4 each.
☐ **SALES ASSISTANT** OK, here you go.
☐ **SALES ASSISTANT** Of course. Enter your PIN, please. OK, here's your receipt. Would you like a bag?
☐ **CUSTOMER** OK, I'd like four white shirts, please.
☐ **CUSTOMER** Can I pay with a card?
☐ **CUSTOMER** Thank you very much.
☐ **CUSTOMER** No, that's OK.
☐ **CUSTOMER** Yes, how much are these white shirts?

d 07.07 Listen and check.

2 PRONUNCIATION Connecting sounds

a 07.08 Listen to the sentences. What are the extra sounds? Check (✓) the correct box.

	/j/	/w/
1 He‿usually wears a white T-shirt.	✓	
2 Is it blue‿or green?		
3 Three‿apples, please.		
4 Are you‿OK?		
5 She‿only wears white.		
6 These cups are for me‿and you.		
7 He‿always wears black.		
8 There are two‿empty bags.		

7C SKILLS FOR WRITING
Good prices!

1 READING

a Read the messages in the chart 1–6. Which advertisement A–D is each message about? Check (✓) the correct box.

Ⓐ **FOR SALE**
Old books, photos, magazines, and newspapers. Very interesting! Good prices.

Ⓑ **FOR SALE**
Beautiful 1960s plates, cups, bowls, and glasses. Not expensive!

Ⓒ **FOR SALE**
Bed, tables, and chairs. I also have some great lamps and pictures for sale.

Ⓓ **FOR SALE**
Men's pants, shirts, jackets, and coats. Very good condition! I also have shoes, umbrellas, and watches for sale.

	A	B	C	D
1 You have an online ad for men's clothes. Do you also sell women's clothes?				✓
2 I saw your online ad for a bed. I'd like to buy it!				
3 I saw your ad. You have some interesting things for sale. How much is the watch? Is it old or new?				
4 I saw your ad for things you want to sell. I'd like to see a photo of the bowls, please.				
5 I have a few questions about the things in your ad. Are the photos in color or black and white? Do you have any magazines in other languages? How old are the newspapers?				
6 I saw your ad. I need four chairs for my apartment. How many do you have? How old are they?				

2 WRITING SKILLS
Commas, exclamation points, and question marks

a Check (✓) the correct ending for the sentences.

1 How much is the …
a ☐ plant, b ☐ plant! c ☑ plant?

2 Good …
a ☐ prices, b ☐ prices! c ☐ prices?

3 Hats for sale: we have …
a ☐ red white green blue and yellow
b ☐ red, white, green, blue, and yellow,
c ☐ red, white, green, blue, and yellow.

4 Can I pay …
a ☐ online, b ☐ online! c ☐ online?

5 Beautiful …
a ☐ bags, and shoes.
b ☐ bags and shoes.
c ☐ bags! and shoes!

6 I'd like to buy …
a ☐ a picture, a bowl, a lamp, and a book.
b ☐ a picture, a bowl, a lamp and a book?
c ☐ a picture, a bowl a lamp and a book

7 How old is …
a ☐ it, b ☐ it! c ☐ it?

8 We need some …
a ☐ cups, plates, and glasses.
b ☐ cups plates and glasses.
c ☐ cups, plates, and glasses?

b Add commas, exclamation points, or question marks to the sentences.

1 How old are you
How old are you?
2 You're a grandmother
____
3 I have a sandwich a drink and a banana.
____
4 These shoes are very expensive
____
5 Where is the bus stop
____
6 Satako Carolina and Beto are in my class.
____

3 WRITING

a Write a response to this ad. You have a new home, and you need furniture, a TV, and a computer.

FURNITURE FOR SALE!
We have chairs, tables, clocks, and technology items for sale. Good condition! Contact Jason.
Reply to this ad

Hi Jason,
____
____
____
____
____
Thanks,
____

UNIT 7
Reading and listening extension

1 READING

a Read the article and match topics a–d to paragraphs 1–4.

a ☐ What I wear when I'm not at work
b ☐ Where I buy my clothes
c ☐ What I wear for special occasions
d ☐ My work clothes

b Read the article again. Are the sentences true or false?

1 Martin's uniform is blue.
2 The police officers' yellow jackets are useful.
3 Martin's friends like fashionable clothes.
4 His favorite color is brown.
5 He has an expensive suit for special events.
6 He usually wears a dark gray shirt for special events.
7 H&M is in the shopping mall.
8 Luciana's favorite store is the same as Martin's.

c Choose someone you know. Write a description of their clothes. Think about these questions:

- What clothes do they wear at different times of the day and different days of the week?
- What are their favorite colors?
- Where do they buy their clothes?

MY CLOTHES by Martin Lopez

1 I don't have to worry about my work clothes. I'm a police officer, and I have a uniform. I like the uniform. We wear a dark blue jacket, dark blue pants, and a white shirt. We also have big yellow police jackets to wear when we're outside on the street. These jackets are very useful because people can see that we are police officers.

2 I'm not very interested in fashion. My wife Luciana says that my clothes are boring, but most of my friends' clothes are the same as mine! When I'm not at work, I like to wear comfortable clothes, for example, jeans and a T-shirt or a sweater. I don't really have a favorite color, but I try not to wear dark blue because it's the color of my uniform. My favorite item of clothing is my old brown jacket.

3 I don't have many expensive clothes, but sometimes I go to special events, for example, when friends get married, and I need to wear something nice. I have a suit by the designer Tom Ford. It has dark gray pants and a matching jacket. I usually wear this with a white shirt and tie.

4 I usually go shopping with Luciana. We both like to go to the shopping mall downtown. It has a lot of stores, and it's easy to find things. My favorite store there is H&M. The clothes at H&M are usually comfortable, and they aren't very expensive. I buy all my clothes there, but Luciana's favorite store is Urban Outfitters.

2 LISTENING

a 07.09 Listen to the conversation. What does the store sell? Underline the correct answer.

books bags computers birthday cards
things for the home clothes chocolates

b 07.09 Listen again. Check (✓) the things the people talk about.

1 a birthday ✓
2 a vacation ☐
3 a party ☐
4 a parent ☐
5 a present ☐
6 a friend ☐
7 a new apartment ☐
8 a new car ☐
9 a birthday card ☐
10 a postcard ☐

c 07.09 Listen again and underline the correct words.

1 Paul thinks shopping is *tiring* / *boring*.
2 Sue wants to buy something *useful* / *colorful*.
3 The cups have pictures of *flowers* / *animals* on them.
4 The lamp is *blue* / *brown*.
5 Paul doesn't like the *color* / *price* of the lamp.
6 Paul's mom wants a table for her *TV* / *laptop*.
7 The table is *$50* / *$60*.
8 Next, Paul and Sue will go to a *café* / *card store*.

d Write about a store you like. Think about these questions:

- What's the store's name?
- Where is it?
- What things do you buy there?
- How often do you go there?
- Why do you like it?

Review

1 GRAMMAR

Check (✓) the sentences that are correct. Correct the mistakes. Remember *near* = here (near me) and *far* = there (not near me).

1 ✓ How much is this chair? (near)
2 ☐ This cups are $6. (near)
3 ☐ That bag is nice. (far)
4 ☐ Those picture is interesting. (far)
5 ☐ I like Martins shoes.
6 ☐ I have two boys. This is the boys' bedroom.
7 ☐ I have one daughter. This is my daughter's hat.
8 ☐ It's Anna's and David's computer.

2 VOCABULARY

Correct the mistakes.

1 I'd like a yellow suitcais.
I'd like a yellow suitcase.
2 He has a red giutar.
3 This pikture is one hundred and sixty-three dollars.
4 Do you have any speekers?
5 It's a light brawn skirt.
6 Where's your green jaket?
7 I have six wite shirts.
8 It's a gray dark coat.

REVIEW YOUR PROGRESS

Look again at Review Your Progress on p. 62 of the Student's Book. How well can you do these things now?
3 = very well 2 = well 1 = not so well

I CAN ...	
talk about things I want to buy	☐
talk about the clothes that people wear	☐
ask about and pay for things in a store.	☐

8A I WAS ON TOUR WITH MY BAND

1 GRAMMAR Simple past: *be*

a Put the words in the correct order to make sentences and questions.

1 last / concert / at / night / was / I / a .
I was at a concert last night.
2 where / morning / this / Nina / was ?
____
3 weren't / last / we / at / night / concert / the .
____
4 they / ago / in / week / were / a / Bogotá .
____
5 week / were / Mexico City / you / in / last ?
____
6 were / yes, / we .
____
7 the / afternoon / at / meeting / was / this / Adrian ?
____
8 no, / wasn't / he .
____

b Complete the conversation with *was, were, weren't,* or *wasn't*.

A You 1 weren't here on Friday afternoon. Where 2__________ you?
B I 3__________ with my brothers. We 4__________ at a basketball game.
A Oh, 5__________ it good?
B No, it 6__________. I don't like basketball.
A Oh. And where 7__________ you on Friday evening?
B We 8__________ at a party.
A 9__________ it a good party?
B It 10__________ OK. The people 11__________ really nice, but the music 12__________ very good.

c 08.01 Listen and check.

2 VOCABULARY Past time expressions

a Complete the sentences with the words in the box.

~~a year ago~~ last month last night
this afternoon this morning yesterday

1 It's January 2021. It was January 2020 a year ago.
2 Today it's Sunday, January third. __________, it was January second.
3 It's Sunday evening. I was at work from 2:00 p.m. until 5:30 p.m. I was at work __________.
4 It's Sunday evening. I was at work from 8:30 a.m. until 11:30 a.m. I was at work __________.
5 It's Sunday. I was at work from 8:00 p.m. until 11:30 p.m. on Saturday. I was at work __________.
6 It's January 2021. I was in Brasília in December 2020. I was in Brasília __________.

b 08.02 Listen and check.

c <u>Underline</u> the correct words.

1 I was in Houston *at* / <u>*on*</u> / *ago* Thursday.
2 **A** Were you in Montreal *yesterday* / *this yesterday* / *on yesterday*?
B Yes, I was.
3 Was Adam at work *on* / *this* / *last* morning?
4 They weren't at home *last* / *ago* weekend.
5 We were at a concert *the last night* / *on last night* / *last night*.
6 Where were you *three months ago* / *ago three months* / *last three months*?

3 PRONUNCIATION *was* / *were*

a 08.03 Listen and <u>underline</u> the two stressed words in each sentence.

1 <u>James</u> was at <u>home</u>.
2 We were in Quito.
3 You were at work.
4 My parents were in Italy.
5 The party was fun.
6 The game was exciting.
7 The concert was good.
8 The meetings were interesting.

8B HE SAW A BEAR

1 GRAMMAR Simple past: affirmative

a Complete the crossword puzzle with the simple past form of the verbs.

➔ Across
2 see
4 look
5 watch
8 come
9 eat
10 have

↓ Down
1 jump
3 walk
5 go
6 try
7 hear
8 call

b Complete the story with the simple past form of the verbs in parentheses.

A Great Evening

My friend Andrés and I [1] went (go) to the movies at 5:30 p.m., and we [2]__________ (watch) a movie. In the movie, a man [3]__________ (play) a video game, and the video game [4]__________ (try) to change him into a robot. It was really interesting!

Then we [5]__________ (go) to the new café on King Street. I [6]__________ (see) Oscar, a man I know from work. We asked him to eat with us, and he [7]__________ (say) yes. Oscar [8]__________ (hear) about the movie, and we [9]__________ (talk) about it. Andrés went home at about 8:30 p.m., but Oscar and I [10]__________ (stay) at the café and [11]__________ (have) coffee.

After that, we went to my house and [12]__________ (play) cards. It was a great evening.

2 VOCABULARY Free time activities

a Complete the activities with the words in the box.

go (x2) have listen to play (x2) read watch take

1 play
the guitar

2 __________
music

3 __________
a shower

4 __________
to the movies

5 __________
a glass of water

6 __________
a magazine

7 __________
a video game

8 __________
a soccer game

9 __________
shopping

b Underline the correct words.

1 I *listen to* / *read* / *watch* the newspaper every day.
2 I sometimes *go* / *listen to* / *watch* movies on TV.
3 I never *go* / *have* / *watch* to the movies.
4 I don't *listen to* / *play* / *read* magazines.
5 I *go* / *take* / *play* a shower every evening.
6 I usually *listen to* / *read* / *watch* a podcast in the morning.
7 I often *read* / *play* / *watch* soccer games on TV.
8 I *have* / *play* / *watch* video games every day.
9 I always *have* / *listen to* / *watch* music in the evening.
10 I always *go* / *play* / *watch* to parties on the weekend.

c 08.04 Listen and check.

3 PRONUNCIATION Sound and spelling: /t/ and /d/

a 08.05 Listen to the simple past verbs. Is the final sound /t/ or /d/? Check (✓) the correct box.

	/t/	/d/
1 talked	✓	☐
2 called	☐	☐
3 tried	☐	☐
4 listened	☐	☐
5 played	☐	☐
6 watched	☐	☐
7 looked	☐	☐
8 lived	☐	☐

8C EVERYDAY ENGLISH
Let's go somewhere this weekend

1 USEFUL LANGUAGE
Making and responding to suggestions

a Complete the sentences and questions with the words in the box.

could   free   ~~idea~~   let's   do you want

1 That's a nice *idea*.
2 ______ go to that new restaurant.
3 ______ to go to the movies?
4 I'm not ______ on Tuesday.
5 We ______ go swimming.

b Underline the correct words to complete the conversation.

ANGELA I went to the beach last week. It was great.
SOL Oh, [1] *let* / *let's* go to the beach together sometime!
ANGELA [2] *That's* / *This is* a great idea.
SOL We [3] *could* / *let's* go this weekend.
ANGELA I'm sorry, I'm [4] *free* / *busy* with my family this weekend.
SOL OK. [5] *Do* / *Are* you want to go next Saturday?
ANGELA I [6] *can't* / *don't* go on Saturday, but I'm [7] *free* / *busy* on Sunday. I can go on Sunday.
SOL [8] *Nice* / *OK*, Sunday. Good.
ANGELA Great!

c 08.06 Listen and check.

d Put the conversation in the correct order.

☐ **SAYEED** Great! Let's go now.
☐ **SAYEED** OK, that's a nice idea! See you at eleven.
☐ **SAYEED** OK. We could go at eleven.
1 **SAYEED** Do you want to go for coffee?
☐ **ANYA** Great! Do you want to go to the new Italian café?
☐ **ANYA** Coffee? Good idea!
☐ **ANYA** I'm sorry, I can't go now. I have a meeting at ten o'clock.

e 08.07 Listen and check.

2 PRONUNCIATION
Sentence stress and intonation

a 08.08 Listen to the sentences. Does the intonation rise (↗) or fall (↘) after the underlined main stress? Check (✓) the correct box.

	↗	↘
1 Do you want to go out for <u>dinner</u> tomorrow?	✓	
2 That's a <u>good</u> idea.		
3 Let's go to the <u>movies</u> next week.		
4 Do you want to go for a <u>walk</u>?		
5 I'm <u>off</u> on Tuesday.		
6 That's a <u>nice</u> idea.		

8C SKILLS FOR WRITING

I want to say thank you

1 READING

a Read the thank you note and texts. Complete the sentences with the names in the box.

~~Charlie~~ Emi Elena Nina Oscar Russell

1 Charlie helped a friend with her apartment.
2 ______ drove to the hospital.
3 ______ helped a friend go shopping.
4 ______ needed to go to the hospital.
5 ______ bought things for her apartment.
6 ______ bought a new dress.

2 WRITING SKILLS
Writing short emails, notes, and texts

a Underline the correct words to complete the email.

[1]*At / For / Dear* Stella,

I [2]*want / was / would want* to say thank you [3]*to / about / for* coming to my concert on Friday. I hope you liked the music. It [4]*be / was / is* good to meet your friends. [5]*I'd like / I hope / I want* we can meet again soon. [6]*There / Here are / Here were* some photos of the evening. I really like the picture of you and Ali!

[7]*See / Talk / Best* you soon,

Ava

b Match 1–6 with a–f to make expressions.

1 [d] Dear
2 [ ] Here are
3 [ ] Thanks for
4 [ ] I hope we can
5 [ ] See you
6 [ ] Talk to

a some photos of the party.
b soon.
c you later!
d Tony,
e see each other again soon.
f your note.

Dear Emi,

Thank you for your help on Wednesday. It was fun to go shopping together, and you helped me find a really nice dress. Now I need some shoes!

See you soon,

Nina

Hi Charlie,
I want to say thanks for your help last weekend. The new table and chairs look really good. I bought some big pictures and lamps on Monday. I hope you can come for dinner some time!
Thanks!

Elena

Hi Oscar,
Here are some chocolates to say thank you for driving me to the hospital on Monday. You were great! I'm home again now, but I'm in bed for a few days. I hope we can meet for coffee soon.

Russell

3 WRITING

a Imagine you had lunch at a friend's house. Write a thank you email to your friend. Remember to give information about:

- the lunch you had
- the people you met
- your photos of the day
- when you hope to see your friend again.

Hi ______,

______

______

______

______

______

______

______

______

______

Talk to you later!

UNIT 8
Reading and listening extension

1 READING

a Read Jill's blog. Are the sentences true or false?

1 Jill was at work on Friday.
2 She lives with Mel and Amy.
3 She was in her office on Sunday.
4 She had coffee with Angela on Sunday.
5 Mel and Amy went to St. Maarten on Monday.
6 Jill and Angela traveled to the airport together.

b Read the blog again. Underline the correct words to complete the sentences.

1 Jill had a *good* / *bad* day at work on Friday.
2 She *went to the theater* / *stayed at home* on Friday evening.
3 She missed the end of the movie because she was *tired* / *bored*.
4 She *watched a cooking show* / *cooked an Indian meal* on Sunday.
5 Angela bought *a suitcase* / *some books* on Sunday.
6 Jill and her friends had pizza for *lunch* / *dinner* on Sunday.
7 They were in the pizza restaurant for *three* / *four* hours.
8 Jill got up *early* / *late* on Monday.
9 Jill and Angela arrived in St. Maarten at *8:30* / *9:30* on Monday.
10 They were in St. Maarten *for vacation* / *on business*.

c Write a blog about your daily life. Write about last week. Think about these questions:

- What did you do?
- Where did you go?
- Who did you see?

80%

FRIDAY JAN 9

I had a bad day at work. The office was really busy. I was so happy to get home. My roommates, Mel and Amy, wanted me to go to the theater with them, but I was tired. They went out, but I watched an old movie on TV in my bedroom. It had a great story, but I fell asleep and don't know how it ended.

SUNDAY JAN 11

I got up late and took a long bath. Then I watched a show about Indian food. I was hungry after the show, so I made a grilled cheese sandwich – my favorite! I met Angela in town for coffee, and then we went shopping. I bought a suitcase for our vacation to St. Maarten, and Angela got some books. At 6:00, we met Mel and Amy for pizza. We were in the restaurant until 10:00!

MONDAY JAN 12

I got up at 4:00 this morning. I was really tired, but our plane to St. Maarten was at 6:30. I went to the airport in a taxi. Angela was already there with the tickets. It only took three hours to travel from Miami to St. Maarten. We had breakfast on the plane. Then Angela read one of her new books, and I looked out the window. We took a tour of the island today, and now we're at the pool. It's amazing!

2 LISTENING

a 08.09 Listen to the conversation. Complete the text with the words in the box.

San Diego	the beach	a concert	work
a restaurant	a museum	~~home~~	the park

Matt

Matt was at [1] _home_ with his kids on Saturday, but his wife was at [2] ______. Yesterday, they all went to [3] ______ in [4] ______.

Grace

Grace and her sister were in [5] ______ over the weekend. They went to [6] ______ on [7] ______ on Saturday and to [8] ______ on Sunday.

b 08.09 Listen again. Who says the sentences? Write *Matt* or *Grace*.

1 I think they were bored. _Matt_
2 ... it wasn't very cold ... ______
3 There were a lot of people there. ______
4 The bands were really good. ______
5 The restaurant was empty! ______
6 A family ticket was only $10.00! ______
7 There weren't any other people. ______
8 It was really interesting. ______
9 There was a lot to see and do. ______
10 It was free. ______

c Write an email to a friend about last weekend. Remember to say:

- where you were
- who you were with
- what you did.

Review

1 GRAMMAR

Correct the mistakes.

1 I am in a meeting yesterday afternoon.
I was in a meeting yesterday afternoon.
2 Emilia not was at work yesterday.
3 We are in the U.S. in 2018.
4 Where they were yesterday?
5 We was play tennis.
6 Jessie arrivd at nine o'clock.
7 I did have breakfast this morning.
8 Carrie goed to New York last year.

2 VOCABULARY

Check (✓) the sentences that are correct. Correct the mistakes.

1 ☐ Where were you ago five years?
Where were you five years ago?
2 ☐ I saw Jeff the last week.
3 ☐ We had a meeting on Monday.
4 ☐ Olivia was here this weekend.
5 ☐ They listened music last night.
6 ☐ I took a shower this morning.
7 ☐ We played computer games last weekend.
8 ☐ We went the movies yesterday.

REVIEW YOUR PROGRESS

Look again at Review Your Progress on p. 70 of the Student's Book. How well can you do these things now?
3 = very well 2 = well 1 = not so well

I CAN ...	
talk about past events	☐
describe events in the past	☐
make and respond to suggestions.	☐

9A I DIDN'T STAY IN A HOTEL

1 GRAMMAR Simple past: negative

a Underline the correct words to complete the text.

@ YOUSSEF'S PLACE, MARRAKESH

Last year, we [1]*don't take / didn't take / didn't took* a vacation here in the U.S. We went to Morocco. We [2]*don't stayed / weren't stay / didn't stay* at a hotel, either. We camped at "Youssef's place" near Marrakesh! We had a big tent with two beds. The campsite was very beautiful, and there were lots of great people there. (We [3]*didn't meet / didn't met / don't met* Youssef, but we met his brother!)

Youssef's place isn't in Marrakesh – it's about 40 minutes from the city. We [4]*not drove / didn't drove / didn't drive* there – we took a taxi. Marrakesh is an exciting city, but we [5]*didn't go / don't went / didn't went* there every day. We visited small towns and villages near the campsite and walked in the mountains.

The vacation wasn't expensive. The tent cost $30 a night, and we usually cooked our meals in the campsite kitchen. But we [6]*don't cook / not cooked / didn't cook* every night! We visited some great restaurants and cafés in Marrakesh.

b Complete the conversations with the simple past negative form of the verbs in parentheses.

1 **A** Our father went to Los Angeles last week. He stayed at a hotel, I think.
  B No, he didn't stay (stay) at a hotel. He stayed in an apartment.

2 **A** We visited a lot of museums on our vacation.
  B We ________ (visit) a lot of museums. We visited two museums! That's not a lot!

3 **A** How was the café?
  B I went to the office! I ________ (go) to a café!

4 **A** They drove their car to the mountains on their vacation.
  B Well, no, they ________ (drive) their car. They took a bus.

5 **A** I bought a few new clothes yesterday.
  B You ________ (buy) a few new clothes! You bought a lot of new clothes!

6 **A** I read a lot of books last weekend.
  B You ________ (read) a lot of books. You read one book! That's all!

c 09.01 Listen and check.

2 VOCABULARY Transportation

a Write the words under the pictures.

bike boat bus car subway plane taxi train ~~tram~~

1 tram

2 ________

3 ________

4 ________

5 ________

6 ________

7 ________

8 ________

9 ________

3 PRONUNCIATION Sound and spelling: the letter *a*

a 09.02 Listen to the words in the box. What sound do the letters in **bold** have? Complete the chart.

~~wh**a**t~~ t**a**xi c**a**r tr**a**m tr**a**in f**a**ther t**a**ke pl**a**ne w**a**tch b**a**g c**a**mp g**a**rden

/æ/ (e.g., *cat*)	/ɑ/ (e.g., *park*)	/eɪ/ (e.g., *plate*)
	what	

9B HOW DID YOU GET THERE?

1 GRAMMAR Simple past: questions

a Put the words in the correct order to make questions.

1 last / did / go / vacation / year / on / where / you ?
Where did you go on vacation last year?
2 you / did / there / how / get ?
____
3 go / friend / a / you / with / did ?
____
4 stay / you / did / where ?
____
5 up / get / what / did / you / time ?
____
6 lot / buy / things / of / you / did / a ?
____
7 did / beach / the / go / you / to ?
____
8 trip / did / enjoy / you / your ?
____

b Complete the conversation with the words in the box.

Did he   was   ~~did~~   did he get   Did Jack stay
Did you   did you stay   he did   he didn't   I didn't

A What [1] ___did___ you do on New Year's Eve? [2] __________ go out?
B No, [3] __________. I stayed at home.
A Really? Why [4] __________ at home?
B I didn't feel very good.
A Oh, no! [5] __________ at home?
B No, [6] __________. He went into the city.
A [7] __________ see the fireworks?
B Yes, [8] __________.
A What time [9] __________ home?
B I don't know. I [10] __________ in bed!

c 09.03 Listen and check.

2 VOCABULARY The seasons and the weather

a Find the four seasons and six weather words.

r	a	i	n	y	j	x	l	y	s
z	y	v	p	x	l	z	z	p	p
f	w	a	r	m	j	q	c	k	r
f	y	p	n	b	h	v	o	d	i
y	j	a	q	k	o	x	l	x	n
c	l	u	s	k	t	v	d	d	g
l	b	t	j	z	h	q	t	p	p
o	f	u	q	s	u	m	m	e	r
u	b	m	v	n	k	t	l	v	z
d	q	n	n	j	p	y	f	t	s
y	x	b	v	t	j	z	y	k	n
q	w	i	n	t	e	r	v	q	o
y	p	s	u	n	n	y	z	j	w

b Underline the correct words to complete the conversations.

1 **A** It's –7 °C! I don't like [1] *summer / winter*!
B Really? I like this season. I like [2] *cloud / cold* weather, and I really like [3] *snowy / snow*!
2 **A** It's really [4] *wind / windy* today.
B Yes, there's always a lot of [5] *wind / windy* in the fall.
3 **A** Look at the [6] *rain / rainy*!
B I know. It often [7] *rains / rainy* in this country.
4 **A** Did you have good weather on your trip? It was 42 °C here.
B 42 °C! No, it wasn't [8] *hot, / cold,* but it was [9] *warm / wind* and [10] *sun / sunny* every day.

c 09.04 Listen and check.

3 PRONUNCIATION Sound and spelling: the letter *o*

a 09.05 Listen to the words in the box. What sound do the letters in **bold** have? Complete the chart.

~~cl**ou**d~~   h**o**t   sn**o**wy   sh**o**pping   t**o**wn   c**o**ld
ph**o**ne   ag**o**   d**o**ctor   br**o**wn   wr**o**ng   h**o**w

/oʊ/ (e.g., *no*)	/aʊ/ (e.g., *now*)	/ɑ/ (e.g., *not*)
	cloud	

9C EVERYDAY ENGLISH
Can you do something for me?

1 USEFUL LANGUAGE
Making and responding to requests

a Complete the conversations with the sentences in the box.

Sorry, I can't. I'm really busy.
Thanks, that's really nice of you.
Sure, no problem.
Can you do something for me?
Oh, OK, I'll do it then.
Could you meet me at the bus station on Sunday?
~~Can you go to the store?~~

Conversation 1

A 1 Can you go to the store? We need bread.
B Sorry, I'm really busy.
A 2 ____________________

Conversation 2

A 3 ____________________
B Sure, what is it?
A 4 ____________________
B Yes, of course.
A 5 ____________________

Conversation 3

A Can you go shopping with me today?
B 6 ____________________
A Oh, OK. Could you come with me tomorrow?
B 7 ____________________
A Thanks.

b 09.06 Listen and check.

c Put the conversation in the correct order.

☐ **KARINA** Can you pick Jenny up from school at four?
1 **KARINA** Hi, Saúl.
☐ **KARINA** See you later.
☐ **KARINA** Thanks, that's really nice of you.
☐ **KARINA** I'm fine, thanks. Could you do something for me?
☐ **SAÚL** Yes, of course. What is it?
☐ **SAÚL** Sure, no problem.
☐ **SAÚL** Hi, Karina. How are you?
☐ **SAÚL** Any time. See you later.

d 09.07 Listen and check.

2 PRONUNCIATION
Syllables and spelling

a 09.08 Listen to the words in the box. How many syllables do they have? Put the words in the correct column.

~~family~~ ~~expensive~~ beautiful station every different museum business favorite camera vegetable difficult

2 syllables	3 syllables
family	expensive

9C SKILLS FOR WRITING

After that, we went to a party

1 READING

a Read three posts online about New Year's Eve and check (✓) the correct people. Sometimes there is more than one possible answer.

	Jiang	Luke	Fernanda
1 Who had dinner in a restaurant?			✓
2 Who had fish for dinner?			
3 Who wore new clothes?			
4 Who met some friends?			
5 Who was with family?			
6 Who watched TV?			
7 Who cleaned the house?			
8 Who saw fireworks?			

What Did You Do Last New Year's Eve?

First, my sisters and I cleaned the house. Then, we went shopping for new clothes. I bought a red dress for New Year's Eve. After that, we cooked fish, vegetables, and rice for dinner. We had a big family New Year's Eve dinner at our home with our parents and grandparents. We didn't go out, but we saw lots of fireworks near our house.

***Jiang**, China*

Like | Reply | Share

First, I went to my brother's apartment, and we watched a movie. We had pizza and ice cream. It was OK. Then, we went into town and met some friends. It was really cold (I only had my old black jeans and T-shirt – no coat or hat!), but we watched the fireworks for about ten minutes. After that, I went home and watched TV.

***Luke**, U.S.*

Like | Reply | Share

First, I had dinner in a restaurant with my friends. I had fish, and it was very good. After that, we went to a party on the beach. It was great! I wore a new white dress. There were a lot of people on the beach. We put flowers in the water and watched the fireworks. After that, we sat and talked until about 4:00 a.m.

***Fernanda**, Brazil*

Like | Reply | Share

2 WRITING SKILLS

Making the order clear

a Underline the correct words to complete the online posts.

What Did You Do on Your Last Birthday?

I'm a doctor, so I was at work during the day – but the evening was fun! [1]*First that, / First,* my friend Tess arrived at my house with a beautiful birthday cake. [2]*After, / Then,* my friend Dave called from New York. [3]*After that, / After,* I met my sister at a Chinese restaurant, and we had a really good dinner.

Anita

1 like

For my last birthday, I went to London with my friend Alan. We went on a boat on the river in the morning. It was nice, but it was very cold! [4]*First, / After that,* we had lunch, and [5]*next that / then* we went to a baseball game. Our team didn't win, but we had a good time anyway!

Ricky

3 likes

Last year, I had a really fun birthday. [6]*First, / Next,* I had lunch with my family. [7]*After then, / Then,* I went shopping with my sister. I bought some clothes and a nice new watch. [8]*After that, / Next time,* I met my friends Iris, Calvin, and Robert. We had dinner and talked all evening.

Wendy

1 like

3 WRITING

a What did you do last New Year's Eve? Write an online post.

UNIT 9

Reading and listening extension

1 READING

a Read the article. Match the people to pictures 1–3.

Billy ☐ Monica ☐ Lucio ☐

1

2

3

b Read the article again. Complete the sentences with *Billy*, *Monica*, or *Lucio*.

1 ___Lucio___ traveled with a friend.
2 __________ wanted to surprise a friend.
3 __________ went on a trip to find a new job.
4 __________ was on vacation.
5 __________ met an important person on a trip.
6 __________ didn't see his or her friend.
7 __________ had a problem because of the weather.
8 __________ didn't arrive at the correct hotel.

c Write about a trip you took. Remember to give information about:

- when the trip was
- why you went on the trip
- where you traveled from and to
- what happened on the trip.

WE ASKED OUR READERS TO SEND IN THEIR TRAVEL STORIES. HERE ARE SOME OF THEM:

Billy, 35

Four years ago, I went to Los Angeles for a job interview. Train tickets were expensive, so I went by bus. The trip took about ten hours. I didn't have anything to read, so I started talking to the woman in the seat next to me. Her name was Alma. We got married last year, and now we have a baby boy!

Monica, 27

I was in the U.S. on business. I had some free time, so I flew to New York to visit my friend Chris. I didn't tell her because I wanted to surprise her. I arrived, but Chris wasn't at home. The man in the apartment next door said she was on vacation! I took a taxi back to the airport, but it started to snow. There were no flights, so I slept at the airport. It was awful!

Lucio, 20

For our vacation, my friend and I decided to spend a week at the beach. We found a nice hotel online and paid for our room. It was a long drive, and we arrived late at night. Then the receptionist said she didn't have a room for us at the hotel. We were so tired! We went to the beach and slept under the stars. The next morning, we realized we went to the wrong hotel!

2 LISTENING

a 09.09 Listen to the interview. Underline the correct words to complete the sentences.

1 The woman is *working* / *on vacation* today.
2 The woman *knows* / *doesn't know* the man.
3 The man and woman met *on vacation last year* / *on the street today.*
4 They talk about the *man's* / *woman's* vacation.

b 09.09 Listen again. Check (✓) the sentences that are true. Correct the false sentences.

1 ☐ Dan's last vacation was in the summer.
Dan's last vacation was in the winter.
2 ☐ He went on vacation with his children.
3 ☐ They traveled by train and car.
4 ☐ They were on vacation for two weeks.
5 ☐ They stayed in an apartment near the beach.
6 ☐ It was their first visit to Miami.
7 ☐ Dan learned some Spanish phrases before his vacation.
8 ☐ Vermont is often cold and snowy in the winter.

c Write a conversation between two friends talking about their last vacation. Think about these questions:

- Where did they go?
- How did they get there?
- Where did they stay?
- How was the weather?

Review

1 GRAMMAR

Check (✓) the simple past sentences that are correct. Correct the mistakes.

1 ☐ **A** Did you take these photos?
B Yes, I took.
Yes, I did.
2 ☐ Where did you go?
3 ☐ I didn't saw Sabine.
4 ☐ What time you arrived?
5 ☐ Elena didn't get up early.
6 ☐ What did they do?
7 ☐ **A** Did you visit your friends?
B No, I didn't visit.
8 ☐ Matt didn't read his emails.

2 VOCABULARY

Correct the mistakes.

1 The weather's very cold and cloud today.
The weather's very cold and cloudy today.
2 We took train to Milan.
3 We went with plane to Cuenca.
4 This is a photo of the snowy in the garden.
5 **A** Did you drive to the beach?
B No, we went by the bus.
6 It always rainy here in the summer.
7 Did you go with car to Medellín?
8 It was suny and warm yesterday.

REVIEW YOUR PROGRESS

Look again at Review Your Progress on p. 78 of the Student's Book. How well can you do these things now?
3 = very well 2 = well 1 = not so well

I CAN ...	
talk about travel and vacation experiences	☐
talk about past vacations	☐
make and respond to requests.	☐

10A WE'RE WATCHING THE GAME

1 GRAMMAR
Present continuous: affirmative

a Underline the correct words to complete the text messages.

1 *I'm cook* / *I'm cooking* / *I cooking* dinner. There's a lot of food. Do you want to eat?

2 *Jaime listening* / *Jaime's listens* / *Jaime's listening* to a podcast. It's really boring!

3 I'm at the station. *It's raining,* / *It raining,* / *It's rain,* and I don't have an umbrella. Can you pick me up?

4 *We're having* / *We having* / *We're have* coffee at the Peach Tree Café. See you soon.

5 *I looking* / *I'm looking* / *I'm look* out the window, and I can see your cat. *It sitting* / *It's sitting* / *It is sit* in a tree!

b Complete the sentences with the present continuous form of the verbs in the box. Use contractions.

go ~~have~~ drink study wear work

1 They 're having dinner.

2 She ____________ coffee.

3 We ____________ to school.

4 I ____________ in the office today.

5 He ____________ a white shirt.

6 You ____________ at the library.

2 VOCABULARY The home

a Complete the crossword puzzle.

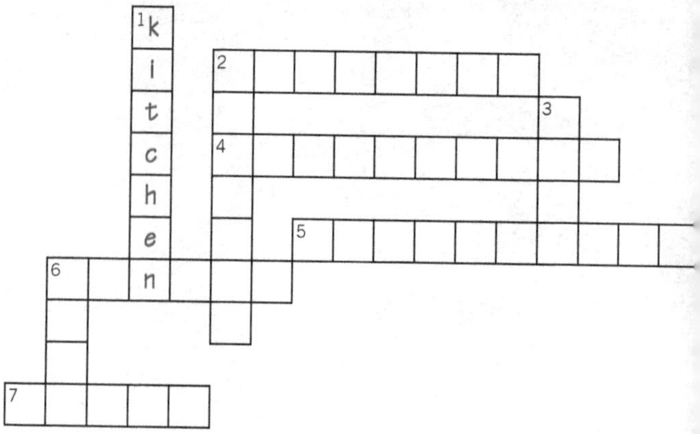

→ Across

2 There's a shower in this room.
4 There's a table and six chairs in this room. We have dinner here every evening. (6, 4)
5 There are a lot of nice chairs and a big TV in this room. (6, 4)
6 Every room has one or more. It's good to open it in hot weather.
7 Every room has one. You can walk or sit there.

↓ Down

1 There's a table and two chairs in this room. I cook and eat here.
2 I read books, listen to music, sleep, and wake up in this room.
3 Every room has one or two. You use it to go in or out.
6 Every room has four or more. You can put pictures there.

3 PRONUNCIATION
Sound and spelling: /tʃ/ and /θ/

a ▶ 10.01 Listen to the words in the box. What sound do the letters in **bold** have? Complete the chart.

~~bathroom~~ kit**ch**en pic**t**ure **ch**air nin**th** mon**th** ques**t**ion **th**irty

/tʃ/ (e.g., lun**ch**)	/θ/ (e.g., ba**th**)
	bathroom

10B ARE YOU WORKING?

1 GRAMMAR Present continuous: negative and questions

a Put the words in the correct order to make sentences and questions.

1 you / are / who / calling ?
Who are you calling?
2 studying / not / we're .
____
3 phone / is / the / Ryan / talking / why / on ?
____
4 not / book / I'm / this / reading .
____
5 are / bus / waiting / for / friends / the / your ?
____
6 the / staying / hotel / not / at / Erica's .
____

b 10.02 Listen and check.

c Complete the conversation with the present continuous form of the verbs in parentheses.

ANDY Hi, it's me. Where are you? What [1]are you doing (you / do)?
TILDA I'm with Renata and Ignacio.
ANDY Oh, [2]_______ (you / work)?
TILDA Yes, we are. Can I have some apple juice, please?
ANDY Apple juice? What [3]_______ (you / talk) about?
TILDA Sorry, [4]_______ (I / not / talk) to you. [5]_______ (I / talk) to the server, but he [6]_______ (not / listen).
ANDY Server? Is there a server at work?
TILDA No, [7]_______ (we / not / work) in the office. We're in a meeting at a café.
ANDY Oh …

d 10.03 Listen and check.

2 VOCABULARY Place phrases with prepositions

a Complete the sentences with *in*, *on*, or *at*.

1 Is Bryan in bed?
2 Sorry, I can't talk now. I'm _______ the airport.
3 Were you _______ school yesterday?
4 Why did you take photos _______ the plane?
5 Angie's _______ the bus stop.
6 Kay and Ellie are _______ vacation.
7 Did you read _______ the train?
8 I talked to Jason _______ the party.
9 Your bag is _______ the car.
10 I saw this comedy _______ the movies last year.
11 Is there Wi-Fi _______ the hotel?
12 I have Wi-Fi _______ home.

b Underline the correct words to complete the conversations.

1 **A** Where are you? Are you *at / in / on* the airport?
B No, I'm *at / in / on* the movies. It's a really good movie!
2 **A** Is Pasha *at / in / on* work?
B No, he's *at / in / on* vacation.
3 **A** You could call Lourdes. She's *at / in / on* home.
B I don't have my phone. It's *at / in / on* the car.
4 **A** Is Allie *at / in / on* school?
B No, she's *at / in / on* bed.
5 **A** Are you *at / in / on* the bus?
B No, there aren't any buses. I'm *at / in / on* a taxi.
6 **A** I'm still *at / in / on* the train station. The train's late.
B Oh. Can you text me when you're *at / in / on* the train?

c 10.04 Listen and check.

3 PRONUNCIATION Sound and spelling: /ə/

a 10.05 Listen and underline the /ə/ sound in each word.

1 husband
2 picture
3 Brazil
4 daughter
5 autumn
6 ago
7 woman
8 correct
9 computer
10 afternoon

10C EVERYDAY ENGLISH

What time's the train?

1 USEFUL LANGUAGE

Asking for travel information

a Complete the expressions with the words in the box.

four o'clock office train ~~six~~ stop ten minutes

1 platform ___six___
2 ticket ________
3 direct ________
4 in ________
5 at ________
6 bus ________

b Complete the conversation with the words in the box.

at can bus stop direct change ~~excuse~~ help problem next ticket

A Oh [1]___excuse___ me!
B Yes? How [2]________ I help you?
A What time's the [3]________ bus to Omaha?
B It's [4]________ 11:15.
A So it leaves in ten minutes. Is it a [5]________ bus?
B No, you [6]________ at Lincoln.
A OK, and which [7]________ is it?
B Number 2, near the [8]________ office.
A Great! Thanks for your [9]________.
B No [10]________.

c 10.06 Listen and check.

d Put the conversation in the correct order.

☐ **B** No problem.
☐ **B** Yes? How can I help?
☐ **B** No, you change at Cincinnati.
1 **A** Excuse me.
☐ **A** What time's the next train to Cleveland?
☐ **B** The next train leaves in half an hour.
☐ **A** So at 10:25. Is it a direct train?
☐ **B** It's platform 9.
☐ **A** OK, and which platform is it?
☐ **A** Great! Thanks for your help.

e 10.07 Listen and check.

2 PRONUNCIATION

Sound and spelling: /ɪə/ and /eə/

a 10.08 Listen to the words in the box. What sound do the letters in **bold** have? Complete the chart.

~~p**ai**r~~ w**ea**r w**e're** z**e**ro y**ea**h r**ea**lly h**ere** ch**air** wh**ere** cl**ear**

/ɪə/ (e.g., *dear*)	/eə/ (e.g., *hair*)
	pair

10C SKILLS FOR WRITING
What time does it start?

1 READING

a Read the messages. Are the sentences true or false?

1 Sandra and Eliana are at the movie theater.
2 Joel wants information about the movie and the movie theater.
3 Sian is walking in the rain.
4 Sian needs information about a soccer game and a concert.
5 Basek isn't driving to the train station.
6 Basek has a ticket for the train.

Joel: Hi Sandra! I'm having lunch with Eliana, and she'd like to come to the movies with us tomorrow. Sorry, I can't remember two things. What time does the movie start? And which movie theater is it? Thanks!

Sian: Hi Brandon. It's a beautiful day here today – very cold but sunny. I'm walking to the mall, and I want to buy something for Gabriel. Can you tell me two things? Does he like soccer? And what kind of music does he like? Thanks!

Basek: Hi Catalina. I'm late for the train, but I'm in a taxi. Two questions: Do you have my train ticket, or do I need to buy a ticket? Which platform does the train leave from? See you soon!

2 WRITING SKILLS
Word order in questions

a Complete the questions. Write one word on each line.

1 **A** How much <u>were</u> <u>the</u> <u>tickets</u>?
B The tickets were $2.50.

2 **A** ______ ______ ______ late?
B Yes, the train's late.

3 **A** He's going home.
B Why ______ ______ ______ home?

4 **A** Where ______ ______ ______ this T-shirt?
B I didn't buy this T-shirt – my brother gave it to me.

5 **A** What time ______ ______ ______ ______?
B The movie starts at 4:45 p.m.

6 **A** Where ______ I ______ a taxi?
B You can get a taxi outside the train station.

7 **A** ______ ______ ______ ______ restaurant?
B Yes, it's an expensive restaurant.

8 **A** ______ ______ ______ ______ parking?
B Yes, the hotel has parking.

b Put the words in the correct order to make questions.

1 from / you / are / where ?
<u>Where are you from?</u>
2 on / Nick / playing / the / computer / is ?
______
3 have / their / how / does / apartment / rooms / many ?
______
4 the / yesterday / give / any / did / teacher / homework / us ?
______
5 can / where / ticket / a / bus / buy / I ?
______
6 he / school / today / at / was ?
______

3 WRITING

a Write a message to another student, and ask for information about your new English class. Ask about:

- the classroom
- the time of the class
- the homework.

______
______
______
______
______
______
______
______
______
______
______
______
______
______
______

UNIT 10
Reading and listening extension

1 READING

a Read the email. Check (✓) the sentences that are true. Correct the false sentences.

1 ☐ Jenny is on vacation in Germany.
   Jenny is on vacation in Japan.
2 ☐ Anna is studying German.
   ____
3 ☐ There are three people in the German family.
   ____
4 ☐ Today is Saturday.
   ____
5 ☐ Anna is in her bedroom right now.
   ____
6 ☐ Most people in the family are outside now.
   ____
7 ☐ Anna wants to know what Martin is doing.
   ____

b Read the email again. Underline the correct words to complete the sentences.

1 *Jenny* / *Anna* / *Anna's parents* organized Anna's trip to Hamburg.
2 It's a *one-week* / *two-week* / *three-week* course.
3 Anna is staying in *a hotel* / *a house* / *an apartment* in Germany.
4 Anna doesn't always *hear* / *understand* / *listen to* what the family members say to her.
5 *Martin* / *Ralf* / *Karl* isn't inside the house right now.
6 Ralf is *studying* / *playing a game* / *texting his parents.*
7 Andrea is *relaxing* / *working* / *helping Martin.*
8 Anna doesn't like Martin's *children* / *food* / *music.*

c Write a description of an evening in your home. Remember to give information about:

- who is in your home
- where each person is
- what each person is doing.

80%

Reply Forward

Hi Jenny,

Thanks for your email. I hope you're enjoying your vacation in Japan. I'm in Hamburg in Germany for two weeks. Mom and Dad sent me here to study German. I didn't really want to come!

I'm staying with a German family here. The parents are Martin and Andrea, and they have two sons, Karl and Ralf. Karl is 17 and Ralf is 14. They're very friendly, but they only speak German, and sometimes I don't understand them.

It's Sunday, and everyone is at home, but we're all in different parts of the house. I'm writing this email in my bedroom. It's really nice because I can see the yard from my window. Karl is in the yard. It's raining, but he's playing with the dog. Ralf is in the room next to me. His parents think he is studying for a test, but he's playing a video game and texting his friends.

Andrea is in the living room. She's a teacher, and she's preparing her lessons for next week. Martin is cooking dinner and listening to some terrible opera music. I don't know what he's making, but he's a great cook. My dad can only make toast!

Anyway, what are you doing? Write and let me know.

Anna

2 LISTENING

a 10.09 Listen. Complete the sentences with the names in the box.

~~Justino~~ Mom Gloria Dad Tim

1 _Justino_ is at home.
2 __________ is at work.
3 __________ is at the sports center.
4 __________ and __________ are at the train station.

b 10.09 Listen again. <u>Underline</u> the correct words to complete the sentences.

1 Justino's dad is <u>*working in*</u> / *calling* his office.
2 Justino is *at home* / *at the movies*.
3 Justino is *watching TV* / *listening to music*.
4 Gloria and her friends *are* / *aren't* at Gloria's house.
5 Justino's mom is with *her husband* / *one of her sons*.
6 Tim's not wearing a *coat* / *sweater*.
7 It's starting to *snow* / *rain*.
8 The train station *is* / *isn't* busy.

c You are somewhere in your hometown. Write a phone conversation between you and a friend. Remember to say:

- where you are
- what you are doing
- what is happening around you.

Review

1 GRAMMAR

Correct the mistakes.

1 I driving to the hospital.
   I'm driving to the hospital.
2 She don't working today.
3 You having lunch?
4 Where Elena going?
5 They're siting in the yard.
6 It raining?
7 No, it not.
8 Yes, is.

2 VOCABULARY

Check (✓) the sentences that are correct. Correct the mistakes.

1 ☐ Is Sofía in the livving room?
   Is Sofía in the living room?
2 ☐ Cara's on vacation.
3 ☐ I'm in the kitchin.
4 ☐ Gaby's at home.
5 ☐ Amber's on the bus.
6 ☐ They're in the dinning room.
7 ☐ She's at a party.
8 ☐ Jorge isn't at bed.
9 ☐ I'm at airport.
10 ☐ We're on a taxi.

REVIEW YOUR PROGRESS

Look again at Review Your Progress on p. 86 of the Student's Book. How well can you do these things now?
3 = very well 2 = well 1 = not so well

I CAN ...	
talk about my home	☐
ask where people are and what they're doing	☐
ask for travel information.	☐

11A SHE WENT AROUND THE EARTH

1 GRAMMAR Object pronouns

a Underline the correct words.

1 Where are the tickets? I had *they* / *them* a minute ago.
2 *We* / *Us* like Joel a lot. He's staying with *we* / *us* this week.
3 This is my sister. *Me* / *I* call *her* / *she* every day.
4 I was on TV. Did you see *I* / *me*?
5 Where's my umbrella? I need *her* / *it*!
6 That man's playing tennis really well. *Him* / *He* is really good. Look at *him* / *he*!
7 **A** Bye, John! Bye, Eva! See *you* / *them* tomorrow!
B Bye!

b Complete the conversation with subject and object pronouns.

A 1 ___I___ have some photos of the party. 2 ________'re really funny.
B Oh, can I see 3 ________?
A Yes, just a minute ... OK ... My brother's in this picture. 4 ________ arrived really late.
B Really? Where is 5 ________? I can't see 6 ________!
A 7 ________'s there, with the blue hat!
B Oh yes! 8 ________'s a very big hat! Is that 9 ________? It's your T-shirt.
A Yes, that's 10 ________. I'm with Ian and Andrea. 11 ________'re really nice.
B And who's that?
A That's Anna-Maria. 12 ________'s at our house now. 13 ________'s staying with 14 ________.
B Can I meet 15 ________?
A Yes, of course. 16 ________ really wants to meet 17 ________!

c 11.01 Listen and check.

2 VOCABULARY Life events

a Write the words under the pictures.

be born die go to school finish college ~~get married~~ go to college grow up have a baby stop working

1 get married

2 ________

3 ________

4 ________

5 ________

6 ________

7 ________

8 ________
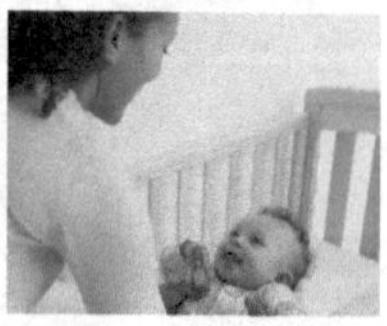
9 ________

b Underline the correct words to complete the text.

Liliana, Rosa, and Me

Liliana 1*was* / *is* born on January 1, 1960 in a small town in Colombia. Her family didn't have much money, but they were very happy. Liliana 2*got to* / *went to* school until she was 16. Then she got a job in an office. She met her husband, Andreas, there. They 3*got* / *had* a baby girl, and they named her Rosa.

Time passed, and Rosa grew 4*on* / *up*. She finished 5*the school* / *school* and went to 6*the college* / *college* in the U.S. She often visited her parents, but she didn't live with them again. Then sadly, Andreas 7*stopped* / *died*. He was only 46. Liliana was very sad, and she 8*ended* / *stopped* working.

Three years ago, Liliana came to the U.S. to be with her daughter, Rosa. I started a conversation with Liliana on a train one day, and two weeks later I met Rosa. Rosa and I 9*got* / *went* married in June!

3 PRONUNCIATION Sound and spelling: numbers

a 11.02 Listen and underline the number you hear.

1	17	70
2	30	13
3	90	19
4	16	60
5	15	50
6	80	18

11B SHE CAN PULL A PLANE

1 GRAMMAR *can* for ability

a Underline the correct words to complete the sentences and questions.

1 Your pictures are beautiful! You ***can*** / *can't* paint very well.
2 **A** *You can / Can you* cook?
   B Yes, *can I / I can.*
3 I like music, but I *can't / can* dance at all. I'm a terrible dancer!
4 Jenny *can to / can* speak Portuguese very well.
5 **A** *Can he / Cans he* run 10 km?
   B No, he *can't / doesn't.*
6 They're good swimmers. They *can swim very well / can very well swim.*

b 11.03 Listen and check.

c Complete the sentences with *can* or *can't* and a verb in the box.

drive play read say ~~speak~~ swim teach write

1 James *can speak* Italian quite well.
2 He goes to the beach every day, but he never goes in the water because he ______________.
3 Their daughter is only four, but she ______________ books.
4 ______________ you ______________ a car?
5 I like children, but I ______________ them. I'm not a teacher.
6 Listen to this! We ______________ "Hello" in Chinese.
7 Look at this! I ______________ "Hello" in German.
8 I'd like to have guitar lessons. I often listen to guitar music, but I ______________ the guitar at all.

2 VOCABULARY Abilities

a Match 1–8 to a–h to make questions.

1 [f] Can you ride
2 [ ] When did you last paint
3 [ ] How often do you cook
4 [ ] You're at a party and you like the music. Do you
5 [ ] Did you sing
6 [ ] Can you run
7 [ ] Do people swim
8 [ ] How often do you drive

a in the ocean in your country?
b dance?
c dinner for a lot of people?
d 5 km?
e a picture?
f a horse?
g a song yesterday?
h a car?

b 11.04 Listen and check.

c Complete the crossword puzzle with simple past verbs.

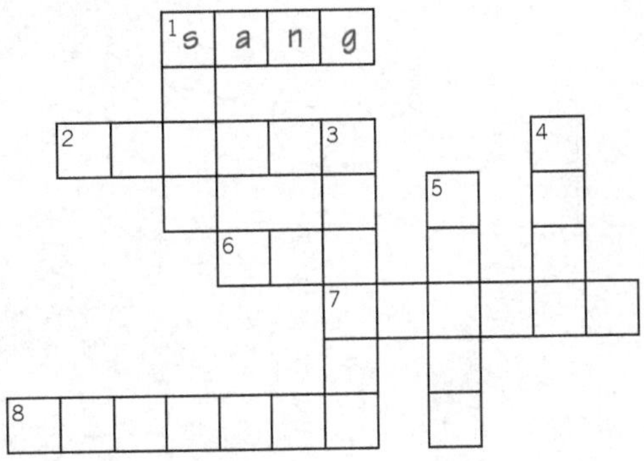

➔ Across
1 In the evening, we sat outside and s*ang* ______________ songs.
2 I p______________ basketball every day when I was in high school.
6 We r______________ 5 km in the park this morning.
7 Ellie c______________ dinner yesterday. It was very good.
8 Gino p______________ a picture of the flowers in the garden.

↓ Down
1 I only s______________ for five minutes because the water was very cold!
3 The music was really good, and we d______________ all night.
4 Damian r______________ his bicycle to school every day last week.
5 I d______________ our new car for the first time yesterday.

3 PRONUNCIATION *can / can't*

a 11.05 Listen to the sentences. Which words are stressed? Check (✓) the correct box.

1 a [ ] **I can** swim.
   b [✓] **I** can **swim**.
2 a [ ] **Can you** drive?
   b [ ] Can you **drive**?
3 a [ ] **Yes**, I can.
   b [ ] **Yes**, I **can**.
4 a [ ] James **can't** sing.
   b [ ] James can't **sing**.
5 a [ ] Can he **dance**?
   b [ ] **Can he** dance?
6 a [ ] **No**, he **can't**.
   b [ ] No, **he** can't.

11C EVERYDAY ENGLISH
What do you think?

1 USEFUL LANGUAGE
Talking about opinions

a Complete the sentences and questions with the words in the box.

idea agree right nice ~~so~~ think favorite

1 I don't think ___so___.
2 Maybe you're ______.
3 I don't think it's a good ______.
4 I think it's really ______.
5 What do you ______?
6 Yes, I ______.
7 That's not my ______.

b Underline the correct words to complete the conversations.

Conversation 1

A [1]What / How do you think of this room?
B I don't [2]*think / agree* gray is a good idea for the walls.
A [3]*You're maybe / Maybe you're* right. But [4]*I / I'm* think it's OK with the red bed.
B I'm not [5]*so / right* sure.

Conversation 2

A What [6]*are / did* you think of the movie?
B It was terrible!
C Yes, [7]*I agree / I'm agree*. It's a really bad movie!
A Really? I don't [8]*think so / think*. I liked it.

c 11.06 Listen and check.

d Complete the conversation with one word on each line. You may use contractions.

MATEO What do you [1]___think___ of my brother's new car?
CARMEN I [2]______ it's really nice.
PHILIP I'm not [3]______ sure.
CARMEN Why not?
PHILIP I [4]______ think yellow is a very good color.
MATEO Maybe you're [5]______.
PHILIP Hmm.
MATEO What [6]______ you think of his old car?

e 11.07 Listen and check.

2 PRONUNCIATION Consonant clusters

a 11.08 Listen and complete the words with the missing letters.

1 touri s t	s t ay
2 e _ _ ineer	e _ _ oy
3 an _ _ er	da _ _ e
4 _ _ _ ool	a _ _
5 thi _ _	ba _ _
6 liste _ _ _	fi _ _
7 clo _ _ _	si _
8 i _ _ eresting	pai _ _

11C SKILLS FOR WRITING

It's a fantastic city

1 READING

a Read the email. Check (✓) the correct answers.

1 What's Yaz doing in Buenos Aires?
  a ☐ She's working and studying.
  b ☑ She's studying.
  c ☐ She's working.

2 What does Yaz think of Buenos Aires?
  a ☐ She likes it, but she thinks it's expensive.
  b ☐ She doesn't like it.
  c ☐ She likes it because it isn't expensive.

3 Why is Yaz in Buenos Aires?
  a ☐ She's learning to play volleyball.
  b ☐ She's learning to dance.
  c ☐ She's studying IT.

4 What can Santiago do?
  a ☐ He can speak other languages.
  b ☐ He can dance.
  c ☐ He can speak other languages and dance.

5 Where did Yaz and Annette meet?
  a ☐ They met in a bookstore.
  b ☐ They met at a volleyball game.
  c ☐ They met in an IT class.

6 How is Yaz feeling?
  a ☐ She's happy because she's not at home.
  b ☐ She's having a good time, but she misses people at home.
  c ☐ She's very sad because she misses her friends and family.

Hi Samuel,

Thanks for your email. It was good to hear from you.

I started college here in Buenos Aires six weeks ago, and it's going really well. The university's fantastic, and Buenos Aires is an exciting city. It's also an expensive city. I'd like to find a job in a store next year because I really need some money!

As you know, I'm studying IT. It's really interesting, and the teachers are good. There's a lot of work to do, but there are also a lot of things to do in my free time. I'm learning to dance, and I can now play volleyball pretty well.

I'm making some new friends here. Santiago and Annette are really nice. I met Santiago at my dance class. He's a language student, and he can speak Spanish, Italian, and German very well. He's also a good dancer, and he helps me in class. Annette is studying IT, and we met in the university bookstore on the first day. We often study together in the evening.

The people here are really nice, but I miss my family at home. I miss my friends, too. Write again soon!

Take care,

Yaz

2 WRITING SKILLS Pronouns

a Read the email. Change the words in parentheses to subject and object pronouns.

Hi Masha,

Thank you very much for your long emails! I read [1] __them__ (*your long emails*) in a café every morning. I like the photos, too. [2] ________ (*The photos*) are very funny!

Things here in Rome are going well. [3] ________ (*Rome's*) a big city with lots of beautiful places to visit. I study at a language school called Accademia Leonardo. [4] ________ (*Accademia Leonardo's*) a really big school, but the classes are small and the teachers are great. My teacher is named Maria. [5] ________ (*Maria's*) a really good teacher, and I like [6] ________ (*Maria*) very much.

I have a new friend named Luigi. He's from Venice. I met [7] ________ (*Luigi*) at a museum! We started talking about the pictures, and then [8] ________ (*Luigi and I*) went out for coffee together.

How are you? Do you see Jess and Otto? I miss [9] ________ (*Jess and Otto*) a lot. And I miss [10] ________ (*Masha*) too, of course!

Write again soon,

Abby

3 WRITING

a Write an email to a friend. Give information about:

- where you are now
- where you study English
- your teacher
- the other students in your class
- what you do in the evening.

Hi ________,

UNIT 11
Reading and listening extension

1 READING

a Read the TV review. Check (✓) the parts of Beth's life you read about.

1 her family ☑
2 her house ☐
3 her school ☐
4 her work ☐
5 her interests ☐
6 her husband's work ☐
7 the death of her husband ☐
8 her children ☐
9 her friends ☐

b Read the review again. Put the events in Beth's life in the order they happened.

☐ Her husband died.
☐ She had a baby.
☐ She went to Haiti.
☐ She finished college.
☐ She started teaching.
☐ She got married.
[1] She left Albany.
☐ She got a job in New York City.

c Choose an interesting member of your family and write about his or her life. Remember to give information about:

- where and when the person was born
- where the person lived
- what work the person did
- the person's family
- why the person was interesting.

LAST NIGHT'S TV

People's Lives is a popular TV show on Channel 12. The show helps people find out about their family history.

Last night, the show was about Fiona Davies and her grandmother, Beth. Fiona didn't know her grandmother well because Beth died when Fiona was two years old. *People's Lives* found out that Beth was from Albany, New York. She was born there in 1922 and had six brothers and sisters. The family was poor, and Beth went to New York City when she was 17. She got a job in a hospital there.

Beth worked at the hospital for six years. Then she studied in college to be a doctor. She was 32 when she finished college and 33 when she married Fiona's grandfather, James. James was a businessman from New Hampshire.

Beth and James were very happy for three years and they had a son, but then James died.

Beth left the U.S. and went to Haiti on a ship with her son. She worked as a doctor there and started a hospital for women. In 1972, Beth returned to Albany to teach at a college there. She taught students who wanted to be doctors. Beth died in Albany in 1984.

It was an interesting show, and Fiona was very happy to know more about her grandmother. Next week, it is Martín Hernández's turn to find out about his grandparents. Don't forget to watch!

- ***People's Lives*, 8 p.m. next Wednesday, Channel 12**

2 LISTENING

a 11.09 Listen to the conversation. Put the jobs in the order that you hear them.

- [ ] chef
- [ ] English teacher
- [ ] receptionist
- [1] singer
- [ ] tour guide

b 11.09 Listen again. Check (✓) the things that Camila can do.

1 sing ☐
2 cook ☑
3 swim ☐
4 speak a foreign language ☐
5 teach ☐
6 speak English ☐
7 drive ☐

c 11.09 Listen again. Underline the correct words.

1 Alex and Camila are *at work* / *at home*.
2 Camila works in *a shop* / *an office* now.
3 *Alex* / *Camila* wants to find a new job.
4 Alex mentions *one job* / *two jobs* on a ship.
5 Camila speaks English and *French* / *Spanish*.
6 Camila doesn't want to live in a very *hot* / *cold* country.
7 Camila *knows* / *doesn't know* a lot about Boston.
8 Camila decides to apply for the job in *Philadelphia* / *Boston*.

d Write a conversation between two friends. One person describes a job he or she would like to do. The other person asks questions. Remember to say:

- what the job is
- why he or she wants to do this job
- why he or she is a good person for this job.

Review

1 GRAMMAR

Correct the mistakes.

1 I have some eggs. We can have it for breakfast.
I have some eggs. We can have them for breakfast.
2 Your dad's an engineer. We could ask her for help.
3 Is your phone new? I like him.
4 Your sister's really nice. How often do you see them?
5 He can to ride a horse.
6 You can drive?
7 I not can sing.
8 **A** Can they swim?
B Yes, they swim.

2 VOCABULARY

Correct the mistakes.

1 Anita and Frank had baby in March.
Anita and Frank had a baby in March.
2 I born in 1995.
3 She was died in 2002.
4 I finished at college last year.
5 I grew in a small town in Ecuador.
6 My father stopped to work last year.
7 She singed a song last week.
8 I rode the car to the train station.
9 I run 10 km last Saturday.
10 We swim in the new swimming pool yesterday.

REVIEW YOUR PROGRESS

Look again at Review Your Progress on p. 94 of the Student's Book. How well can you do these things now?
3 = very well 2 = well 1 = not so well

I CAN ...	
talk about people's lives	☐
talk about things I know how to do	☐
talk about opinions.	☐

12A I'M GOING TO TAKE A LONG HOT BATH

1 GRAMMAR
be going to: affirmative and negative

a Underline the correct words to complete the conversations.

Conversation 1

A Is there an email from Esteban? [1]*He going to* / *He's going to* / *He's going* write to you with information about the boat trip.

B I don't know. [2]*I'm going not to* / *I'm not going to* / *I'm not going* check my email today or tomorrow.

A Oh, OK. Well, I'm going [3]*to call* / *calling* / *call* him this evening, so I can ask him then.

Conversation 2

A My vacation starts tomorrow! [4]*I go to* / *I'm going* / *I'm going to* sleep for ten hours every night! [5]*I going* / *I'm going* / *I'm go* to watch TV every day!

B Really? That's so boring! My brother and I [6]*am going* / *is going* / *are going* to work on a farm near the mountains. The people there [7]*are going* / *is going* / *am going* to teach us how to ride horses.

A Hmm, sounds interesting. What about your sister?

B [8]*She's going not* / *She not going* / *She isn't going* to come with us. She wants to stay at home.

b 12.01 Listen and check.

c Complete the sentences with the *be going to* form of the verbs in the box.

cook	do	~~play~~	(not) ride	(not) sing
(not) stay	take	(not) use	watch	

1 We ___are going to play___ volleyball tomorrow.
2 My sister ________________ dinner for me tonight.
3 I ________________ a song!
4 Samantha ________________ yoga this afternoon.
5 They ________________ at expensive hotels.
6 Luis ________________ his motorcycle fast.
7 I ________________ a long, hot bath.
8 We ________________ a movie on TV tonight.
9 You ________________ your phone in the restaurant!

2 VOCABULARY
Months and future time expressions

a Check (✓) the correct ending for the sentences.

1 They're going to get married ...
a ☐ on June. b ☐ June. c ☑ in June.

2 It's Juan's birthday ...
a ☐ in Friday. b ☐ this Friday. c ☐ at Friday.

3 I have a test ...
a ☐ at Wednesday. b ☐ next Wednesday.
c ☐ in Wednesday.

4 See you ...
a ☐ in Monday. b ☐ at Monday.
c ☐ on Monday.

5 Can you call me ...
a ☐ this afternoon? b ☐ on afternoon?
c ☐ next afternoon?

6 He's going to finish school ...
a ☐ in three weeks. b ☐ this three weeks.
c ☐ on three weeks.

7 See you ...
a ☐ on tomorrow. b ☐ tomorrow.
c ☐ in tomorrow.

8 We're going to visit Alia and Ahmed ...
a ☐ on the weekend. b ☐ in the weekend.
c ☐ the weekend.

9 See you ...
a ☐ at the fall! b ☐ on the fall!
c ☐ in the fall!

10 She's going to stop working ...
a ☐ in month. b ☐ at month.
c ☐ next month.

3 VOCABULARY Ordinal numbers

a 12.02 Listen and write the ordinal numbers.

1st	first	5th	______	16th	______
2nd	______	9th	______	20th	______
3rd	______	12th	______	22nd	______
4th	______	13th	______	31st	______

4 PRONUNCIATION
Sentence stress: *be going to*

a 12.03 Listen and underline the stressed words in the sentences.

1 You're going to stay at a hotel.
2 They're going to live in Canada.
3 Anna's going to do her homework.
4 I'm going to check my email.
5 He's going to listen to music.
6 I'm going to read a book.

12B WHAT ARE YOU GOING TO DO THIS WEEKEND?

1 GRAMMAR *be going to*: questions

a Put the words in the correct order to make questions.

1 coffee / to / meet / when / are / we / going / for ?
When are we going to meet for coffee?
2 at / lunch / to / is / going / home / have / he ?
______
3 where / married / to / get / going / they / are ?
______
4 you / train station / to / to / are / the / drive / tomorrow / going ?
______
5 to / do / she / evening / going / this / what's ?
______
6 going / potatoes / you / how / are / cook / to / the ?
______

b 12.04 Listen and check.

c Complete the sentences with the *be going to* form of the verbs in parentheses.

1 **A** What are you going to do (you / do) this morning?
B I ______ (clean) the house – and you ______ (help) me!
2 **A** So, ______ (he / play) the piano this evening?
B Yes, he is. ______ (you / listen)?
3 **A** What ______ (you and your friends / do) on vacation?
B I don't know. We ______ (talk) about it this afternoon.
4 **A** Where ______ (she / watch) TV?
B In the living room.
5 When ______ (I / do) all these things on my list?

d 12.05 Listen and check.

2 VOCABULARY Common verbs and collocations

a Match 1–8 with a–h to make sentences.

1	[h] I'm going to make	a	my homework today.
2	[ ] I'm not going to do	b	shopping tomorrow.
3	[ ] I want to clean	c	Violet in the hospital.
4	[ ] I'd like to paint	d	a picture of you.
5	[ ] We can go	e	the car. It's really dirty.
6	[ ] I don't use	f	to the party.
7	[ ] I'm going to visit	g	my phone every day.
8	[ ] We're going to invite Carlos	h	a cake for my mom.

b Complete the crossword puzzle.

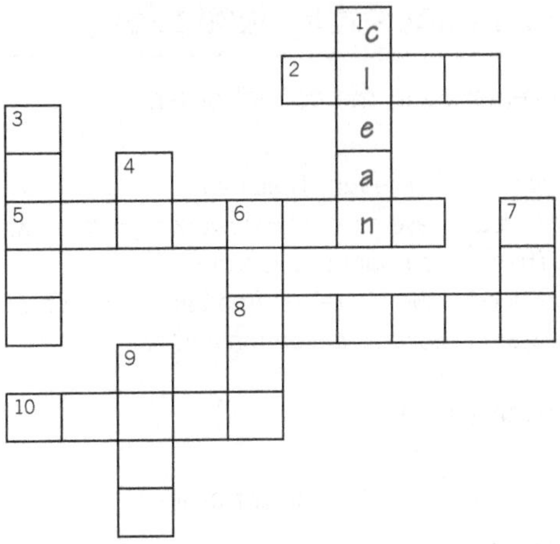

→ Across

2 I p______ sports every day. My favorite sports are running, swimming, and soccer.
5 Did you make plans to go s______ at the mall this weekend?
8 I'm going to i______ Pedro to my apartment to play video games.
10 I have so many ideas I want to write about. I'm going to s______ a blog.

↓ Down

1 I'm going to clean ______ the apartment today. It's a mess.
3 They went to Colombia, but they didn't v______ Bogotá.
4 I'd like to g______ for a walk this afternoon.
6 I didn't p______ my room red. The walls are still white.
7 Can I u______ your computer?
9 I'm going to m______ some coffee. Would you like some?

3 PRONUNCIATION Sound and spelling: /v/ and /w/

a 12.06 Listen to the words in the box. Do they have the /v/ sound or the /w/ sound? Complete the chart.

~~wall~~ evening Wi-Fi visit November volleyball warm drive windy winter weekend invite

/v/	/w/
	wall

12C EVERYDAY ENGLISH
Do you want to watch the game?

1 USEFUL LANGUAGE
Making and accepting invitations

a Put the conversation in the correct order.

- [ ] **B** Yes, I am.
- [ ] **B** Sure, that sounds like fun. Thank you.
- [ ] **B** I'd like to, but I have a lot of homework for tomorrow.
- [ ] **A** Great! Then do you want to see a movie?
- [ ] **A** You're a good student! Are you free tomorrow night?
- [1] **A** Do you want to go to a concert tonight?

b 12.07 Listen and check.

c Put the conversation in the correct order.

- [1] **A** Do you want to come for dinner tomorrow night?
- [ ] **A** Great! You can come on Saturday.
- [ ] **A** Are you free on Friday?
- [ ] **B** No, sorry. I'm busy on Friday, too. But Saturday's OK.
- [ ] **B** Thanks!
- [ ] **B** Sorry, I'm busy then.

d 12.08 Listen and check.

e Complete the conversations with the words in the box.

can go do free busy
~~want~~ thank OK sounds to

Conversation 1

A Do you 1 ___want___ to come to my party on Saturday?
B Sure, that 2 __________ like fun. Thank you.

Conversation 2

A 3 __________ you want to go to the movies on Thursday?
B Sorry, I'm 4 __________ then. But Friday's 5 __________.
A OK, we 6 __________ go on Friday.
B Great!

Conversation 3

A Do you want to 7 __________ to lunch this weekend?
B I'd like 8 __________, but I'm out of town this weekend.
A Are you 9 __________ next weekend?
B Yes, I am.
A We can go then!
B 10 __________ you. That sounds great.

f 12.09 Listen and check.

2 PRONUNCIATION
Sound and spelling: *oo*

a 12.10 Listen to the words in the box. What sound do the letters *oo* have? Complete the chart.

~~book~~ pool good school food
boots cook look afternoon

/uː/ (e.g., *soon*)	/ʊ/ (e.g., *foot*)
	book

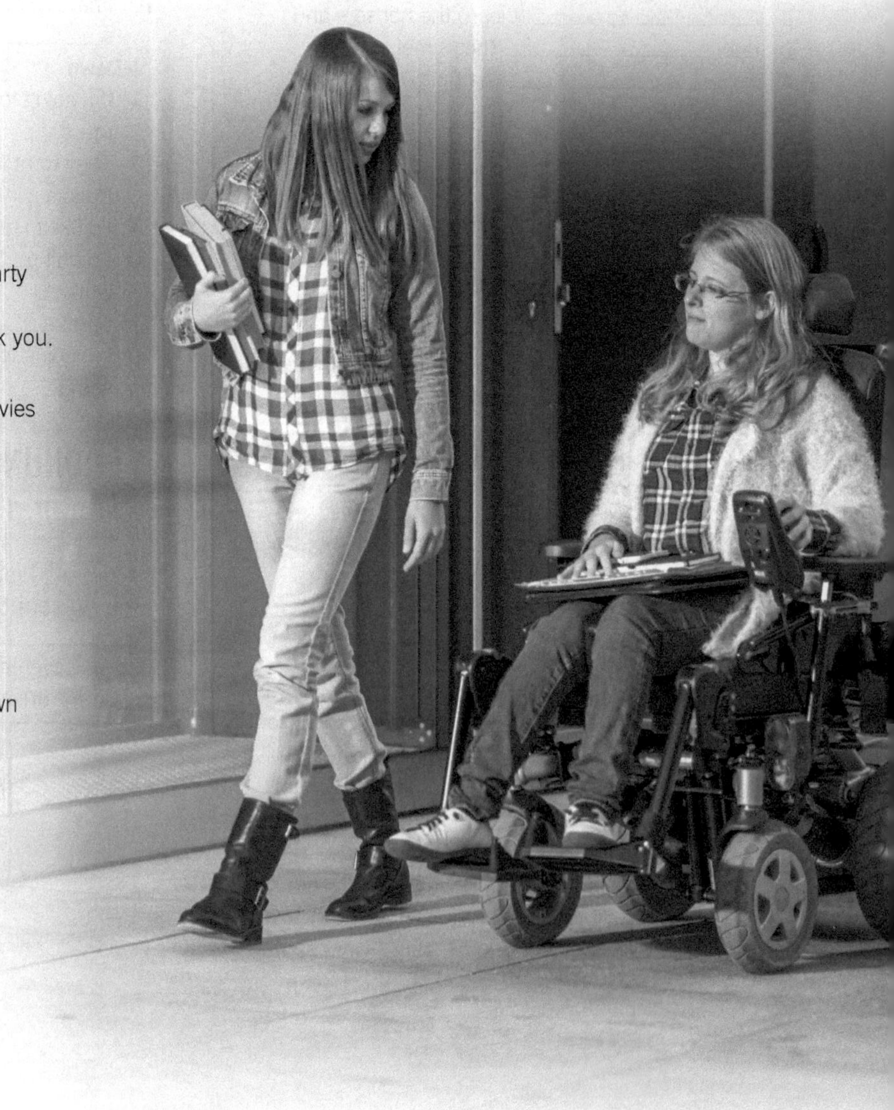

12C SKILLS FOR WRITING
I'm free next weekend

1 READING

a Read the invitations and replies. Are the sentences true or false?

1 Eddy and Hugo are going to have pizza together tonight.
2 Eddy is going to make the pizza.
3 They're going to talk on the phone at 2:30 this afternoon.
4 Hugo is free at 7:30 this evening.
5 Nerissa wants to go shopping in town on Tuesday morning.
6 Selena and Nerissa are going to see each other this Tuesday.
7 Selena can go to Nerissa's apartment this Wednesday.
8 Selena can go to Nerissa's apartment next Wednesday.

Hi Hugo!

How are you? Do you want to meet for dinner today – at about 6:30? There's a new pizza place near the bus station. People say it's really good. I can call you this afternoon – at about 2:30. Is that OK with you?

Talk to you soon!

Eddy

Hi Eddy,

I'm good, thanks. Pizza tonight sounds great, but I'm busy at 6:30. Is 7:30 OK for you? I'm going to be at work this afternoon, but we could talk around 5:30.

Hugo

Hi Selena,

Do you want to come over to my apartment on Tuesday morning? We could do some online clothes shopping together, and I can make lunch.

I hope to see you then!

Nerissa

Hi Nerissa,

That's a great idea, but I'm out of town until Friday. Maybe we could do it next Tuesday? I'm free next Wednesday, too.

Talk to you soon!

Selena

2 WRITING SKILLS Paragraphs

a Put the text in the correct order to make Ethan's email invitation.

☐ Paul's staying with me this week, and he can play the guitar really well. We could eat and then sing songs. What do you think? Are you free on Saturday?
☐ I hope you can come!
☐ Hi Juan,
☐ I'm thinking about having a barbecue at my house on Saturday evening – chicken, fish, vegetables, things like that. Would you and Ada like to come?
☐ Ethan

b Put the text in the correct order to make Juan's reply to Ethan's email invitation.

☐ Is 8:00 OK? Would you like us to bring some food?
☐ Juan
☐ See you on Saturday!
☐ Thank you, that sounds great. We're busy on Saturday afternoon, but we can come in the evening.
☐ Hi Ethan,

3 WRITING

a Write a reply to the invitation.

Hi!

How are you? I'm going to the beach this Saturday. Do you want to come with me? We can swim, relax in the sun, and play volleyball.

We could go in the morning or the afternoon. What do you think? Maybe some of your friends would like to come, too.

Hector

Hi Hector,

UNIT 12
Reading and listening extension

NEW YEAR, NEW ME
by Matt Simpson

1 Today is January 1st – a good day to start my new life! Some people talk about changing their lives, but they don't do anything. I'm not going to talk about changing my life. I have a list of things I want to do, and I'm going to do all of them.

2 What am I going to do first? Well, I usually get up, go to work, come home, have dinner, and then watch TV until it's time to go to bed. I never get any exercise. Starting tomorrow, I'm going to get up early every day and go for a run. I'm also going to use the swimming pool at the gym after work.

3 I'm not going to stay at home every evening. I'm going to go online to get some information about language courses. I'm interested in Spanish. I also want to take a cooking class. I don't know how to cook, so I usually eat at restaurants or buy pizza. On the weekend, I go to my mom's house for meals!

4 I spend a lot of money on clothes, but I'm not going to shop for them anymore. I'm going to put my money in the bank. My brother and I want to travel and see new places. We're planning to leave our jobs in September and travel around the world.

5 Those are my plans. What are YOU going to do to change your life this year?

1 READING

a Read the blog. Match the ideas a–e to paragraphs 1–5.

a ☐ Traveling to new places
b ☐ Asking about another person's plans
c ☐ Learning new things
d ☐ Deciding to change
e ☐ Changing a daily routine

b Read the blog again. Check (✓) the activities Matt is going to do.

1 buy more clothes ☐
2 cook a meal for his mom ☐
3 do a lot of traveling ☐
4 get a new job ☐
5 use the gym ☑
6 learn to swim ☐
7 learn to cook ☐
8 play soccer at the gym ☐
9 run every day ☐
10 save money ☐
11 study a foreign language ☐
12 walk to work every day ☐

c Imagine it's a new year and you want to change your life. Make a list of things you're going to do and things you aren't going to do.

I'm going to ...	I'm not going to ...

2 LISTENING

a 12.11 Listen to the video call. Match the activities in the box with the people. Complete the notes.

have dinner   meet friends   play tennis   read a book   see a soccer game   go to the movies   spend a day at Disneyland   take the dog for a walk   ~~visit a movie studio~~

Fernanda
visit a movie studio
____
____

Bruno
____
____
____

Mom
____
____

Dad
____

b 12.11 Listen again. Are the sentences true or false?

1 Fernanda and Bruno are brother and sister.
2 Fernanda is in the U.S.
3 She is traveling by train.
4 She was in San Diego yesterday.
5 Rodeo Drive is famous for its stores.
6 The soccer game is on Thursday.
7 The next place Fernanda plans to visit is Las Vegas.
8 Fernanda is going to call her parents on the weekend.

c Write a conversation between two friends. One person is going to visit a big city. The other person asks about his or her plans. Remember to say:

- which city he or she's going to visit
- how he or she's going to travel
- what he or she's going to do and see there.

Review

1 GRAMMAR

Check (✓) the sentences that are correct. Correct the mistakes.

1 ☑ Eduardo isn't going to sleep here tonight. He's at a hotel.
2 ☐ They're going play volleyball. Do you want to watch them?
3 ☐ Are you going to take a bath?
4 ☐ What we are going to do now?
5 ☐ **A** Is he going to work in a bank?
B Yes, he's going.
6 ☐ **A** Is she going to go to college?
B No, she isn't.
7 ☐ I'm going not to get up early. I'm going to stay in bed until lunchtime!
8 ☐ When I going to see you again?

2 VOCABULARY

Correct the mistakes.

1 See you on the two of March.
See you on March second.
2 They're going to visit João on the summer.
3 It's August twelve.
4 I'm going to start work in Monday.
5 He was born on Februry fifteenth.
6 My clothes are dirty. I need to make laundry.
7 We could visit Leo and Craig to the party. They love parties!
8 I don't really like to play sports, but I make yoga every day.
9 I want to clean the walls green.
10 Can I do the computer for five minutes? I need to check my email.

REVIEW YOUR PROGRESS

Look again at Review Your Progress on p. 102 of the Student's Book. How well can you do these things now?
3 = very well   2 = well   1 = not so well

I CAN ...	
talk about future plans	☐
ask and answer about future plans	☐
make and accept invitations.	☐

AUDIOSCRIPTS

Unit 1

01.01

A Hi. I'm Horacio. What are your names?
B Hi. I'm Carmen.
C And I'm Camila.
A Are you from the U.S.?
B No, we're from Spain. We're Spanish.

01.02

1 **A** This is my friend Francisca.
B Where's she from? Is she Brazilian?
A No, she's not. She's from Colombia.
2 **C** Who are Javier and Guillermo? Are they baseball players?
D No, they're not. They're soccer players.
C Are they American?
D No, they're not. They're Mexican.

01.03

1 British
2 Colombian
3 Chinese
4 Italian
5 Brazilian
6 Canadian
7 Japanese
8 Spanish
9 American
10 Mexican

01.04

1 **SELENA** Good morning! How are you today?
AYLA I'm not bad, thanks. And you?
SELENA I'm OK, thanks.
2 **HOLLY** Good afternoon, Dean.
DEAN Hi, Holly. This is my friend Natasha.
HOLLY Hi, Natasha. How are you?
NATASHA I'm good, thank you. Nice to meet you.

01.05

CARLA Good afternoon. My name's Carla Ortega.
JAMES Hello. I'm James Hargreaves.
C Nice to meet you, James.
J Nice to meet you, too.
C Oh, Aman! This is James Hargreaves from Blue Web Technology.
AMAN Hello, James! How are you?
J I'm fine, thank you. And you?
A I'm good, thanks.

01.06

1 **A** How are you?
2 **B** I'm fine, thanks.
3 **A** So, this is your office.
4 **B** Good morning!
5 **A** I'm Andy and this is Ernesto.
6 **B** Nice to meet you.

01.07

BEN Good morning. Is this the teachers' room?
ANNIE Yes, it is. Are you a new student?
B No, I'm not. I'm a new teacher.
A Oh, are you Ben?
B Yes, Ben Curtis.
A It's nice to meet you, Ben. I'm Annie Costa, the school director.
B Nice to meet you, too.
A Where are you from, Ben?
B Seattle, Washington.
A Really? Seattle's a nice city.
B Yes, it is. And you?
A I'm from New York.
B New York is great.
A Well, your class is 1A.
B OK.
A This is the class list. It's a small class. There are eight students.
B What countries are they from?
A Let's see. Hmmm.... Paulo and Helena are from Brazil. Lee and Ping are from China. Daniela is from Ecuador, and Manuel is Colombian.
B And Simona and Gianna. Those are Italian names. Are they from Italy?
A Yes, that's right. OK, this is your desk, and here are your books.

Unit 2

02.01

1 where
2 he
3 what
4 who
5 his
6 her
7 hello
8 when

02.02

1 I have eighty books.
2 Thirty apples, please.
3 I have six bags.
4 Twelve eggs, please.
5 Do you have fifty tickets?
6 Fourteen bottles of water, please.

02.03

1 knives
2 keys
3 students
4 newspapers
5 tickets
6 books
7 watches
8 bottles
9 houses

02.04

A What's your last name?
B It's Milner.
A How do you spell that?
B M-I-L-N-E-R.
A What's your address?
B It's 39 Oak Street, Buffalo, New York.
A What's your phone number?
B It's (716) 555-3214.

02.05

A What's your last name?
B It's Ramirez.
A How do you spell that?
B R-A-M-I-R-E-Z.
A What's your phone number?
B It's (619) 555-9867.
A What's your email address?
B It's m-ramirez-one-one-eight at travelmail dot com.

02.06

1 How are you?
2 Is it a small town?
3 What's your last name?
4 What's your address?
5 Can you spell that?
6 What's the spelling?
7 Are you from a big city?
8 Is this your phone?
9 Where are you from?
10 What's your email address?

02.07

DARREN I'm Darren. I'm the manager of a TV store in Boston. I don't have an office, but I have a chair and a desk in the store. It's an old desk and it's not big, but I have a phone, a computer, and a newspaper on my desk, and the keys to the store.
PAULA I'm Paula. I'm a teacher in Washington. I have three desks! One is at home, one is in the teachers' room at the school, and one is in my classroom. I have a laptop and some books on my desk in the teachers' room, but I don't have a phone. Today, my bag is on my desk with my umbrella.
JAMIE I'm Jamie. I'm a student in a small town called West Valley. I have a desk at school and another desk in my bedroom where I do my homework. I have a computer on my desk at home, and today I also have an apple, a knife, and a glass of water.

Unit 3

03.01

1 We eat fruit every day.
2 Do you eat bread?
3 They don't eat eggs.
4 **A** Do you like vegetables?
B No, I don't.
5 Do you like fish?
6 **A** Do you like meat?
B No, we don't.
7 I don't like rice.
8 **A** Do you like fruit?
B Yes, I do.

03.02

DUNCAN Mmm! I like meat! I eat meat every day!
RAJIT Really? I don't eat meat.
D Oh, you don't eat meat. Do you eat fish?
R No, I don't.
D Do you eat eggs?
R Yes, I do. I like eggs.

03.03

1 my
2 tea
3 this
4 rice
5 milk
6 is
7 I
8 we
9 like
10 Italy
11 meat
12 key

03.04

1 **A** What fruit do you like?
B Apples and bananas.
2 **A** Would you like a cookie with your coffee?
B No, thanks.
3 **A** A tomato is a vegetable.
B No, it's not. It's a fruit!
4 **A** We have bread, butter, and eggs.
B Good! An egg sandwich for me, please.
5 **A** A cheese pizza, please.
B Certainly.
6 **A** Is this fruit juice?
B Yes, it's orange juice.

03.05

1 eight o'clock
2 quarter after seven
3 eleven o'clock
4 quarter after one
5 ten thirty
6 quarter to one
7 quarter to six
8 one thirty

03.06

1 morning
2 afternoon
3 half
4 after
5 four
6 class
7 banana
8 store

03.07

SERVER Good morning.
NAOMI Hello. I'd like a piece of banana bread, please.
S Sure. And to drink?
N Can I have a large coffee?
S Of course. With milk?
N No, thanks.
S Here you go. That's $6.50, please.
N OK. Thank you very much.
S Thank you.

03.08

SERVER Good afternoon.
COLBY Hello. I'd like a tea, please.
S Sure. And to eat?
C I'd like a cheese sandwich.
S With tomato?
C No, thanks. And can I have some chocolate cake and a bottle of water too?
S Of course! That's $11, please.
C OK. Here you go.
S Thank you.

03.09

1 a slice of pizza
2 a large coffee
3 a bottle of water
4 a slice of cheese
5 a small orange juice
6 a large tea
7 a glass of milk
8 a piece of chocolate cake

03.10

ANNA What do you want, John?
JOHN A sandwich. What sandwiches do they have?
A They have cheese.
J Oh, I never eat cheese. I don't like it.
A Really? Do you like eggs?
J Oh, yes. I like eggs.
A And tomatoes?
J Yes, I eat a lot of tomatoes.
A OK. They have egg and tomato sandwiches. I like those.
J Great. So, two egg and tomato sandwiches.
A Do they have any cake?
J Yes, they have chocolate cake or apple pie with ice cream.
A Well, I don't eat a lot of chocolate, but I like chocolate cake.
J Me, too. And to drink? Tea or coffee? I usually drink tea.
A I don't like hot drinks. Do they have fruit juice?
J Yes, apple juice or orange juice.
A Oh, apple juice. I always have orange juice for breakfast.
J OK. Excuse me. Could we please get two orders ...

Unit 4

04.01

1 Where do you live?
2 Do you speak French?
3 Do you work in a factory?
4 What do you study?
5 Do you go to the gym?
6 When do you have lunch?

04.02

1 she
2 that
3 right
4 father
5 mother
6 three
7 they
8 the
9 eight
10 brother

04.03

KATIE Do you have photos of your home?
AMY Yes, I do.
K Can I see them?
A Sure. This is my apartment.
K Who's this?
A My brother Harry.
K Great photo!
A Thanks. Here's another picture of my apartment.
K It's really nice.

04.04

JENNY Do you have photos of your family?
HUGO Yes, I do.
J Can I see them?
H Sure. This is my dad and my brother. And this is me with my mom and my sister.
J Nice picture! They look like you!

04.05

1 orange
2 question
3 cheap
4 page
5 child
6 Japan
7 Germany
8 manager
9 picture
10 watch

04.06

PHILIP Hi, Kerry!
KERRY Hello, Philip. It's so nice to see you! How are you?
P I'm fine, thanks. I live here, in Boston. I'm a student at Boston University now.
K Really? What subject do you study?
P Business.
K Do you like it?
P I love it.
K And where do you live?
P In a house with two other students. And you?
K I live in Hong Kong now, and I work in an office at the university.
P Really? Do you speak Chinese?
K Just a little bit. I'm taking Chinese classes in the evenings. I mostly speak English at work.
P So why are you in Boston now?
K I'm on vacation. I'm here to see my family.
P How are your mom and dad?
K They're well, thanks. How are your parents?
P They're fine. They live in France now, near Paris.
K Wow, that's great. Hey, look, is that Ali over there? Ali! ... Ali! ...

Unit 5

05.01

1 There's one school here.
2 There are two teachers.
3 There are a few cars.
4 There's a small museum.
5 There are ten families.
6 There's an old hospital.

05.02

1 few
2 butter
3 sometimes
4 supermarket
5 school
6 study
7 beautiful
8 pool
9 love
10 who
11 funny
12 mother

05.03

1 **A** Is there a bathtub in the room?
B No, there isn't. But there is a shower.
2 **A** There aren't any hotels in this town.
B Oh.
A There's a hostel on Maple Street. It's really good.
B OK. Thanks.
3 **B** Is there parking at this hotel?
A Yes, there is. And it's free.
B Are there any empty rooms on the first floor?
A No, there aren't. Sorry. But there are a lot of empty rooms on the top floor.
B Oh. No thanks.

05.04

1 bath
2 shower
3 China
4 Russia
5 she
6 sure
7 six
8 finish
9 museum
10 shop
11 station
12 movies

05.05

A Excuse me, can you help me?
B Yes, of course.
A Is there a movie theater near here?
B No, I'm sorry. There aren't any movie theaters near here. But there are two downtown.
A OK. And is there a museum near here?
B Yes, there is. It's on this street. Just over there.
A Oh yes! Great! Thanks for your help.
B No problem.

05.06

A Excuse me, can you help me?
B Yes, of course.
A Are there any hotels near here?
B Yes, there are. There's one on the next street.
A Oh, good. And are there any hostels – cheap hostels?
B No, I'm sorry. There aren't.
A OK. Thanks for your help.
B No problem.

05.07

1 It's a very good hotel.
2 It's so hot today!
3 I'm really sorry.
4 This room's really nice.
5 It's a very big school.
6 This TV is so old!
7 The museum's really boring.
8 The bathroom's very small.

05.08

RECEPTIONIST Good morning. Can I help you?
YUSUF Hi, yes. I'd like a hotel room for the weekend.
R Well, there are a lot of different hotels, and they have different prices.
Y I'd like a room for one person near the beach.
R Hmm, it's summer and there aren't a lot of empty rooms. The Hotel Splendor is near the beach. They have rooms with bathtubs for $160 a day, and breakfast is free. The rooms have TVs and Wi-Fi, and there's a good restaurant in the hotel.
Y It's very expensive. I don't have a lot of money.
R Well, there's the Star Hostel near the train station. The rooms are small, but they're clean. A room for one person is only $40.
Y That's cheap.
R Yes, it is. There are showers in all the rooms and Wi-Fi in the café on the first floor, but you have to pay for the Wi-Fi. A lot of backpackers stay there, and it's very friendly.
Y Is there a restaurant?
R No, there isn't. But there's the café, and there are two big supermarkets near the hostel.
Y OK.
R Do you want the phone number for the hostel?
Y Yes, please.

Unit 6

06.01

1 Hello, I'm Natasha. I'm the hotel receptionist.
2 **A** What's your brother's job?
B He's a businessman.
3 I'm an IT worker. I work with computers.
4 I'm a taxi driver. I sometimes work at night.
5 I work at this restaurant. I'm a chef.
6 Lionel Messi is a soccer player.
7 **A** Does your sister work at Bank One?
B Yes, she's a bank teller.
8 **A** Excuse me! Are you a doctor?
B Yes, I am. Can I help you?

06.02

1 The children are in the kitchen.
The machine accepts cash.
This chair is cheap.
2 She finishes work late.
Please wash the dishes.
Nachos have cheese and chips.
3 I'd like a chicken sandwich, please.
The receptionist is at the bus station.
The child plays at the beach.
4 Check the chart.
She's very special to me.
Our teacher likes chocolate cake.
5 The chef is short.
Please share the information.
He chooses chicken at the supermarket.

06.03

1 **A** Where does Lottie live?
B In Germany.
2 **A** Does your husband work at night?
B No, he doesn't.
3 When does Martin get home?
4 Can I call your sister tomorrow morning? What time does she wake up?
5 When do Kathy and Jim finish work?
6 **A** Does he study English?
B Yes, he does.

06.04

1 I wake up at 7:00 a.m., and I get up at 7:15 a.m.
2 I have breakfast at home.
3 I go to work every day.
4 I start work at 9:00 a.m., and I finish work at 5:30 p.m.
5 I arrive home at 6:30 p.m.
6 I go to bed at 11:00 p.m.

06.05

1 twenty
2 breakfast
3 Spanish
4 play
5 fruit
6 class

06.06

MAX Would you like a cup of coffee?
EVA Yes, please.
M And would you like a piece of cake?
E No, that's OK, thanks.
M Hmm... I need to go to the store. There isn't any coffee here!
E I'll come with you.
M That's great, thanks. And I need to make the cake... I don't have any!
E I'll help you.
M Thank you. That's very nice of you.

06.07

UMA Would you like a cup of coffee, Raul?
RAUL Yes, please.
U And would you like a piece of cake?
R No, I'm fine, thanks – just coffee, please.
U I need to make lunch for José and Karina.
R I'll help you.
U All right. Thanks. We need pizzas.
R I can make pizzas. I make very good pizzas!
U Don't worry. It's OK. The pizzas at the supermarket are fine.
R OK, I'll go to the supermarket.
U Thank you. That's great.

06.08

1 **A** I need to make dinner for eight people!
B I can help you.

2 **A** I need to go to the supermarket, but I'm really busy.
B I'll go.
3 **A** Oh no! I don't have any money with me!
B I can pay.
4 **A** I can't open this bottle of water!
B I'll do it.
5 **A** I need to go to the store. Can you drive me?
B Sorry, but I'm really busy. Jim can take you.
6 **A** I need some cups. Do you have any cups?
B No, I don't. I can give you some glasses.

06.09

PRESENTER Welcome to the show. This week we're talking to people who live and work in the state of Michigan. Today, my guest is 44-year-old Ian Baker. Which part of Michigan are you from, Ian?
IAN I'm from a town outside Detroit.
P And what do you do?
I Well, I'm a businessman. My wife Rita and I have a factory near Detroit
P That's interesting. How many people work there?
I We have 90 workers.
P And what do you make?
I We make computers for schools.
P Do you like your work?
I Yes, I do. I work long hours. I start at 7 or 8 in the morning and finish at 7 or 8 in the evening. But my job is never boring. I'm not in my office every day. I go to different places and I meet a lot of people, like the teachers and children who use our computers.
P Are all your customers here in the U.S.?
I No, some customers are here, but schools in South America also buy our computers, so I often fly to Brazil for meetings.
P Are your meetings in English?
I Sometimes, but we usually speak in Portuguese.
P Does your wife go with you?
I No, she works with our customers in the U.S. and Canada.
P And how often do you meet together ...

Unit 7

07.01

1 Do you like these flowers?
2 Do you like those flowers?
3 I'd like that car.
4 I want this car!

07.02

1 This glass is ten dollars and fifty cents.
2 This soccer ball is thirty dollars.
3 That guitar is one hundred and twenty-nine dollars.
4 That picture is twenty-four dollars and seventy-five cents.
5 Those cups are nine dollars and fifty cents.
6 These plants are three dollars and eighty-nine cents.

07.03

1 ball	5 plate	9 cup
2 suitcase	6 lamp	10 plant
3 glass	7 guitar	
4 bag	8 book	

07.04

1 It's Kate's bag.
2 They're Darren's shoes.
3 My friend's jacket is brown.
4 The boys' pants are new.
5 I never wear jeans.
6 I sometimes wear my sister's clothes.

07.05

1 jeans	5 nationality	9 Germany
2 large	6 Japanese	10 sure
3 fashion	7 vegetables	11 gym
4 shoes	8 shirt	12 shop

07.06

1 **A** That's $52.95, please.
B Can I pay with a card?
A Yes. Enter your PIN, please.
2 **A** Can I help you?
B No, thanks. Can I look around?
A Of course.
3 **A** Here's your receipt.
B Thanks.
4 **A** How much are these bags?
B They're $35 each.
5 **A** I'd like that T-shirt, please.
B Sure. Here you go.

07.07

SALES ASSISTANT Hi! Can I help you?
CUSTOMER Yes, how much are these white shirts?
SA They're $4 each.
C OK, I'd like four white shirts, please.
SA Sure. That's $16, please.
C Can I pay with a card?
SA Of course. Enter your PIN, please. OK, here's your receipt. Would you like a bag?
C No, that's OK.
SA OK, here you go.
C Thank you very much.
SA Thank you.

07.08

1 He usually wears a white T-shirt.
2 Is it blue or green?
3 Three apples, please.
4 Are you OK?
5 She only wears white.
6 These cups are for me and you.
7 He always wears black.
8 There are two empty bags.

07.09

PAUL Why do we have to go shopping, Sue? It's so boring.
SUE You know why, Paul. It's your mom's birthday on Sunday. We need to find a present for her.
P That's easy. I always buy a box of chocolates and some flowers from that store near the train station.
S Chocolates and flowers? Those are boring. Let's get something useful for her new apartment.
P All right. Well, let's try this store here. They sell lots of nice things.
S OK. Look, these cups and plates are nice. They have pictures of cats on them.
P Mom has a lot of cups. I don't think she needs any more.
S Well, what about a clock? Those clocks over there are nice ... Or how about a new lamp? This one is good for reading, and your mom loves reading.
P A lamp is a good idea. I don't like the color, though. Do they have any other colors?
S I don't think so. They're all brown.
P Oh, right ... Hey, do you like those little red tables over there? I know Mom wants a new table for her laptop.
S That's a good idea. How much are they?
P Looks like they're $60 each.
S Let's get one. And next, we need to go to the card store and choose a birthday card.

Unit 8

08.01

A You weren't here on Friday afternoon. Where were you?
B I was with my brothers. We were at a basketball game.
A Oh, was it good?
B No, it wasn't. I don't like basketball.
A Oh. And where were you on Friday evening?
B We were at a party.
A Was it a good party?
B It was OK. The people were really nice, but the music wasn't very good.

08.02

1 It's January 2021. It was January 2020 a year ago.
2 Today it's Sunday, January third. Yesterday, it was January second.
3 It's Sunday evening. I was at work from two p.m. until five thirty p.m. I was at work this afternoon.
4 It's Sunday evening. I was at work from eight thirty a.m. until eleven thirty a.m. I was at work this morning.
5 It's Sunday. I was at work from eight p.m. until eleven thirty p.m. on Saturday. I was at work last night.
6 It's January 2021. I was in Brasília in December 2020. I was in Brasília last month.

08.03

1 James was at home.
2 We were in Quito.
3 You were at work.
4 My parents were in Italy.
5 The party was fun.
6 The game was exciting.
7 The concert was good.
8 The meetings were interesting.

08.04

1 I read the newspaper every day.
2 I sometimes watch movies on TV.
3 I never go to the movies.
4 I don't read magazines.
5 I have a shower every evening.
6 I usually listen to a podcast in the morning.
7 I often watch soccer games on TV.
8 I play video games every day.
9 I always listen to music in the evening.
10 I always go to parties on the weekend.

08.05

1 talked	5 played
2 called	6 watched
3 tried	7 looked
4 listened	8 lived

08.06

ANGELA I went to the beach last week. It was great.
SOL Oh, let's go to the beach together some time!
A That's a great idea.
S We could go this weekend.
A I'm sorry, I'm busy with my family this weekend.
S OK. Do you want to go next Saturday?
A I can't go on Saturday, but I'm free on Sunday. I can go on Sunday.
S OK, Sunday. Good.
A Great!

08.07

SAYEED Do you want to go for coffee?
ANYA Coffee? Good idea!
S Great! Let's go now.
A I'm sorry, I can't go now. I have a meeting at ten o'clock.
S OK. We could go at eleven.
A Great! Do you want to go to the new Italian café?
S OK, that's a great idea! See you at eleven.

08.08

1 Do you want to go out for dinner tomorrow?
2 That's a good idea.
3 Let's go to the movies next week.
4 Do you want to go for a walk?
5 I'm off on Tuesday.
6 That's a nice idea.

08.09

GRACE Morning, Matt. How was your weekend?
MATT Hi Grace. It was good, thanks. My wife was at work on Saturday, so I was at home with the kids. I think they were bored. But we went to a concert in the park yesterday. There were a lot of people there.
G Really? How was the concert?
M It was fun. The bands were really good.
G Was it expensive?
M Well, that was the best thing. A family ticket was only $10.00! We had a great day. There was a lot to see and do. Anyway, how was your weekend?
G Oh, it was good. I was in San Diego.
M Wow! Was it your first time there?
G No, my sister moved there four years ago, and I visit her often.
M Was it hot?
G It wasn't hot, but it wasn't very cold either. On Saturday, we went to a restaurant on the beach. We had a great meal there, but the restaurant was empty! There weren't any other people.
M What did you do yesterday?
G We went to the Natural History Museum. It was really interesting. We saw so many things.
M How much was it?
G It was free. You don't have to pay to go into some museums on Sunday.

Unit 9

09.01

1 **A** Our father went to Los Angeles last week. He stayed at a hotel, I think.
B No, he didn't stay at a hotel. He stayed in an apartment.
2 **A** We visited a lot of museums on our vacation.
B We didn't visit a lot of museums. We visited two museums! That's not a lot!
3 **A** How was the café?
B I went to the office! I didn't go to a café!
4 **A** They drove their car to the mountains on their vacation.
B Well, no, they didn't drive their car. They took a bus.
5 **A** I bought a few new clothes yesterday.
B You didn't buy a few new clothes! You bought a lot of new clothes!
6 **A** I read a lot of books last weekend.
B You didn't read a lot of books. You read one book! That's all!

09.02

1 what	5 train	9 watch
2 taxi	6 father	10 bag
3 car	7 take	11 camp
4 tram	8 plane	12 garden

09.03

A What did you do on New Year's Eve? Did you go out?
B No, I didn't. I stayed at home.
A Really? Why did you stay at home?
B I didn't feel very good.
A Oh, no! Did Jack stay at home?
B No, he didn't. He went into the city.
A Did he see the fireworks?
B Yes, he did.
A What time did he get home?
B I don't know. I was in bed!

09.04

1 **A** It's –7°C! I don't like winter!
B Really? I like this season. I like cold weather, and I really like snow!
2 **A** It's really windy today.
B Yes, there's always a lot of wind in the fall.
3 **A** Look at the rain!
B I know. It often rains in this country.
4 **A** Did you have good weather on your trip? It was 42°C here.
B 42°C! No, it wasn't hot, but it was warm and sunny every day.

09.05

1 cloud	5 town	9 doctor
2 hot	6 cold	10 brown
3 snowy	7 phone	11 wrong
4 shopping	8 ago	12 how

09.06

1 **A** Can you go to the store? We need bread.
B Sorry, I'm really busy.
A Oh, OK, I'll do it then.
2 **A** Can you do something for me?
B Sure, what is it?
A Could you meet me at the bus station on Sunday?
B Yes, of course.
A Thanks, that's really nice of you.
3 **A** Can you go shopping with me today?
B Sorry, I can't. I'm really busy.
A Oh, OK. Could you come with me tomorrow?
B Sure, no problem.
A Thanks.

09.07

KARINA Hi, Saúl.
SAÚL Hi, Karina. How are you?
K I'm fine, thanks. Could you do something for me?
S Yes, of course. What is it?
K Can you pick Jenny up from school at four?
S Sure, no problem.
K Thanks, that's really nice of you.
S Any time. See you later.
K See you later.

09.08

1 family	5 every	9 favorite
2 expensive	6 different	10 camera
3 beautiful	7 museum	11 vegetable
4 station	8 business	12 difficult

09.09

Researcher Excuse me, sir. Do you have time to answer a vacation survey?
Dan Uh, yes. OK.
R Thank you. And what is your name?
D My name's Dan.
R Hi, Dan. My first question is: Do you live here in Vermont, or are you on vacation?
D I live here, actually.
R When was your last vacation?
D Last winter. My wife and I went to Miami. Our children didn't want to come, so they stayed home.
R How did you get there?
D Well, my wife doesn't like flying, so we went by train. We also rented a car in Miami, so we didn't need to take taxis.
R How long was your vacation?
D Three weeks.
R Did you stay in a hotel?
D No, we didn't. One of our friends has a house near the beach, and we stayed there. It was our second time there.
R What did you do on your vacation?
D My wife and I took a Mexican cooking class. The teacher told us how to say the names of food in Spanish and even taught us a few Spanish phrases. It was fun.
R Why didn't you go to another country for your vacation?
D Because Miami has great weather! Vermont is cold and snowy in the winter, and Miami is warm. The sky is clear and blue, and we wear shorts —in January! You can't beat that.
R I agree! OK, one last question ...

Unit 10

10.01

1 bathroom	5 ninth
2 kitchen	6 month
3 picture	7 question
4 chair	8 thirty

10.02

1 Who are you calling?
2 We're not studying.
3 Why is Ryan talking on the phone?
4 I'm not reading this book.
5 Are your friends waiting for the bus?
6 Erica's not staying at the hotel.

10.03

ANDY Hi, it's me. Where are you? What are you doing?
TILDA I'm with Renata and Ignacio.
A Oh, are you working?
T Yes, we are. Can I have some apple juice, please?
A Apple juice? What are you talking about?
T Sorry, I'm not talking to you. I'm talking to the server, but he's not listening.
A Server? Is there a server at work?
T No, we're not working in the office. We're in a meeting at a café.
A Oh ...

10.04

1 **A** Where are you? Are you at the airport?
B No, I'm at the movies. It's a really good movie!
2 **A** Is Pasha at work?
B No, he's on vacation.
3 **A** You could call Lourdes. She's at home.
B I don't have my phone. It's in the car.
4 **A** Is Allie at school?
B No, she's in bed.
5 **A** Are you on the bus?
B No, there aren't any buses. I'm in a taxi.
6 **A** I'm still at the train station. The train's late.
B Oh. Can you text me when you're on the train?

10.05

1 husband	6 ago
2 picture	7 woman
3 Brazil	8 correct
4 daughter	9 computer
5 autumn	10 afternoon

10.06

A Oh, excuse me!
B Yes? How can I help you?
A What time's the next bus to Omaha?
B It's at 11:15.
A So it leaves in ten minutes. Is it a direct bus?
B No, you change at Lincoln.
A OK, and which bus stop is it?
B Number two, near the ticket office.
A Great! Thanks for your help.
B No problem.

10.07

A Excuse me.
B Yes? How can I help?
A What time's the next train to Cleveland?
B The next train leaves in half an hour.
A So at 10:25. Is it a direct train?
B No, you change at Cincinnati.
A OK, and which platform is it?
B It's platform nine.
A Great! Thanks for your help.
B No problem.

10.08

1 pair	4 zero	7 here	9 where
2 wear	5 yeah	8 chair	10 clear
3 we're	6 really		

10.09

JUSTINO Hi, Mom.
MOM Hello, Justino. Is Dad home yet?
J No, there's no one here except me. Dad called from his office half an hour ago. There's a problem, so he's working late.
M What are you doing? I can hear music. Are you watching TV?
J No, I'm listening to music and getting ready to go out to the movies.
M And where's Gloria?
J She's at the sports center with some of her friends. I think they're playing tennis. What about you?
M I'm at the train station with your brother. We're waiting for the train, but there's a problem.
J What do you mean?
M Well, the train is late, and it's starting to snow now.
J Oh, no!
M Tim's not very happy. He's only wearing his jeans and a sweater. He didn't want to put his coat on when we left the house.
J Can I talk to him?
M Not now. He's in the café. He's buying some hot drinks for us.
J Oh, right.
M Oh, I have to go! The train is coming. There are a lot of people here on the platform, and it's going to be difficult to get a seat. Tim! Tim! Hurry up!

Unit 11

11.01

A I have some photos of the party. They're really funny.
B Oh, can I see them?
A Yes, just a minute ... OK ... My brother's in this picture. He arrived really late.
B Really? Where is he? I can't see him!
A He's there, with the blue hat!
B Oh yes! It's a very big hat! Is that you? It's your T-shirt.
A Yes, that's me. I'm with Ian and Andrea. They're really nice.
B And who's that?
A That's Anna-Maria. She's at our house now. She's staying with us.
B Can I meet her?
A Yes, of course. She really wants to meet you!

11.02

1 seventeen	4 sixteen
2 thirty	5 fifty
3 ninety	6 eighteen

11.03

1 Your pictures are beautiful! You can paint very well.
2 **A** Can you cook?
B Yes, I can.
3 I like music, but I can't dance at all! I'm a terrible dancer!
4 Jenny can speak Portuguese very well.
5 **A** Can he run 10 km?
B No, he can't.
6 They're good swimmers. They can swim very well.

11.04

1 Can you ride a horse?
2 When did you last paint a picture?
3 How often do you cook dinner for a lot of people?
4 You're at a party, and you like the music. Do you dance?
5 Did you sing a song yesterday?
6 Can you run 5 km?
7 Do people swim in the ocean in your country?
8 How often do you drive a car?

11.05

1 I can swim.	4 James can't sing.
2 Can you drive?	5 Can he dance?
3 Yes, I can.	6 No, he can't.

11.06

1 **A** What do you think of this room?
B I don't think gray is a good idea for the walls.
A Maybe you're right. But I think it's OK with the red bed.
B I'm not so sure.
2 **A** What did you think of the movie?
B It was terrible!
C Yes, I agree. It's a really bad movie!
A Really? I don't think so. I liked it.

11.07

MATEO What do you think of my brother's new car?
CARMEN I think it's really nice.
PHILIP I'm not so sure.
C Why not?
P I don't think yellow is a very good color.
M Maybe you're right.
P Hmm.
M What did you think of his old car?

11.08

1 tourist	stay	5 think	bank
2 engineer	enjoy	6 listened	find
3 answer	dance	7 clocks	six
4 school	ask	8 interesting	paint

11.09

ALEX What are you doing, Camila?
CAMILA Hi Alex. I'm working.
A You're looking at job websites! I hope your manager doesn't see you.
C He's not in the office.
A Good! Let me see the website. Look! There's a job for a singer on a ship ... but you can't sing. Oh, and there's a job for a chef on the same ship. You're a fantastic cook.
C Just one small problem. I can't swim, so I don't want to work on a boat.
A Well, what about this job as an English teacher in Mexico? You speak Spanish, and you love traveling.
C But I can't teach and I don't want to live in a really hot country.
A Oh, right. Well, an IT company in Philadelphia wants a receptionist.
C I don't want to work in another office.
A How about this job as a tour guide? You take people on bus tours around Boston.
C Hmm ... Sounds interesting. What do they want?
A Someone who knows a lot about Boston and who can speak English and another language.
C Well I was born in Boston, so I know a lot about it, but I can't drive.
A You don't drive the bus. You just talk to the passengers.
C Oh, right. Well, that sounds interesting. I'll call the tour company this afternoon!
A Shhh! Your manager's coming back.

Unit 12

12.01

1 **A** Is there an email from Esteban? He's going to write to you with information about the boat trip.
B I don't know. I'm not going to check my email today or tomorrow.
A Oh, OK. Well, I'm going to call him this evening, so I can ask him then.
2 **A** My vacation starts tomorrow! I'm going to sleep for ten hours every night! I'm going to watch TV every day!
B Really? That's so boring! My brother and I are going to work on a farm near the mountains. The people there are going to teach us how to ride horses.
A Hmm, sounds interesting. What about your sister?
B She's not going to come with us. She wants to stay at home.

12.02

first	fifth	sixteenth
second	ninth	twentieth
third	twelfth	twenty-second
fourth	thirteenth	thirty-first

12.03

1 You're going to stay at a hotel.
2 They're going to live in Canada.
3 Anna's going to do her homework.
4 I'm going to check my email.
5 He's going to listen to music.
6 I'm going to read a book.

12.04

1 When are we going to meet for coffee?
2 Is he going to have lunch at home?
3 Where are they going to get married?
4 Are you going to drive to the train station tomorrow?
5 What's she going to do this evening?
6 How are you going to cook the potatoes?

12.05

1 **A** What are you going to do this morning?
B I'm going to clean the house – and you're going to help me!
2 **A** So, is he going to play the piano this evening?
B Yes, he is. Are you going to listen?
3 **A** What are you and your friends going to do on vacation?
B I don't know. We're going to talk about it this afternoon.
4 **A** Where's she going to watch TV?
B In the living room.
5 When am I going to do all these things on my list?

12.06

1 wall	5 November	9 windy
2 evening	6 volleyball	10 winter
3 Wi-Fi	7 warm	11 weekend
4 visit	8 drive	12 invite

12.07

A Do you want to go to a concert tonight?
B I'd like to, but I have a lot of homework for tomorrow.
A You're a good student! Are you free tomorrow night?
B Yes, I am.
A Great! Then do you want to see a movie?
B Sure, that sounds like fun. Thank you.

12.08

A Do you want to come for dinner tomorrow night?
B Sorry, I'm busy then.
A Are you free on Friday?
B No, sorry. I'm busy on Friday, too. But Saturday's OK.
A Great! You can come on Saturday.
B Thanks!

12.09

1 **A** Do you want to come to my party on Saturday?
B Sure, that sounds like fun. Thank you.
2 **A** Do you want to go to the movies on Thursday?
B Sorry, I'm busy then. But Friday's OK.
A OK, we can go on Friday.
B Great!
3 **A** Do you want to go to lunch this weekend?
B I'd like to, but I'm out of town this weekend.
A Are you free next weekend?
B Yes, I am.
A You can come then!
B Thank you. That sounds great.

12.10

1 book	4 school	7 cook
2 pool	5 food	8 look
3 good	6 boots	9 afternoon

12.11

FERNANDA Hi, Bruno. Can you hear me?
BRUNO Hi, Fernanda. Yes, I can see you and hear you. Where are you now?
F I'm in Los Angeles for three days. I took the bus from San Francisco yesterday.
B What are you going to do there?
F Well, today after breakfast, I'm going to visit a movie studio and go shopping on Rodeo Drive.
B Wow! Rodeo Drive is expensive.
F I just want to look around. Maybe I'll see someone famous! What about you?
B It's not raining here, so I'm going to take the dog for a walk. Then I'm going to have dinner and read a book.
F What about Mom and Dad? Are they at home with you?
B Mom's here, but she's in the shower. She's going to meet some friends later and go to the movies. Dad went out a few minutes ago. He's going to play tennis with Uncle Mike.
F Oh, right.
B Anyway, tell me the rest of your plans.
F Well, tomorrow morning I'm going to go to the beach, and in the afternoon I have a ticket for a soccer game. But Thursday is the best day. I'm going to spend the day at Disneyland!
B Wow! That sounds fantastic.
F It is – the U.S. is great! After Los Angeles, I'm going to take a bus to Las Vegas, and after that, Dallas and New Orleans.
B Well, have a good time.
F Thanks, Bruno. Tell Mom and Dad I'll call them tomorrow.
B Will do! They'll be happy to hear from you. Bye!
F Bye!

ANSWER KEY

Unit 1

1A

1

a 2 I'm 3 You're not 4 We're 5 am I 6 I'm not 7 I am 8 we're not

b 2 We're not teachers. 3 I'm not from Ecuador. 4 Are you OK? 5 How are you? 6 Are we in the U.S.?

2

a Brazil, China, Italy, Japan, Australia, Mexico, Canada

b 2 Italy 3 Japan 4 Ecuador 5 Colombia 6 the U.S. 7 Spain 8 China

3

a I'm I'm I'm we're We're

1B

1

a 2 they are 3 Are, they're not 4 Is she, is 5 he's not

b 2 is 3 Is 4 's not 5 's 6 are 7 Are 8 're not 9 're 10 Are 11 're not 12 're

2

Across: 2 American 3 Australian 4 Italian 5 Ecuadorian 6 Chinese
Down: 1 Brazilian 7 Spanish 8 Canadian 9 Japanese

3

a 2 syllables: Chinese, Spanish
3 syllables: Japanese, Mexican, Italian, Brazilian
4 syllables: Canadian, Colombian, American

1C

1

a 2 bad 3 you 4 OK 5 afternoon 6 This 7 are you 8 thank 9 to meet

c 2 My 3 I'm 4 Nice 5 too 6 is 7 Hello 8 thank 9 And 10 thanks

2

a 2 a 3 a 4 b 5 b 6 b

1C Skills for Writing

1

a 2 a 3 a 4 b 5 b 6 a

2

a 2 Alfonso 3 Italian. 4 friends 5 Emma. 6 They're 7 Spain 8 Emma 9 American.

b 2 This is Diana. 3 My teacher is Canadian. 4 Their apartment is in New Orleans. 5 I'm from Mexico. 6 We're American. We're from Seattle.

3

a Sample answer:

Hi, my name's Tamara. I'm from Spain. I'm a student in New York, in the U.S. My friends aren't Spanish, and they aren't American. Lia is Chinese, and Kurt is from Germany. Ana and Lucas are from Brazil.

Reading and listening extension

1

a a 4 b 2 c 1 d 3

b True: 2, 4, 5, 7 False: 1, 3, 6, 8

2

a Brazil, China, Italy, Ecuador, Colombia

b 2 at work 3 Ben 4 Washington 5 New York 6 1A 7 Ecuadorian 8 Italian

Review

1

2 **A** Where are you?
3 I'm not a student. I'm a teacher.
4 **A** And who is this?
5 These are my friends. They're Ecuadorian.
6 What's your name?
7 We're not Italian. We're Mexican.
8 Where is Sue from?

2

2 ✓
3 He's from Canada.
4 ✓
5 We're Brazilian.
6 Are you Spanish?
7 ✓
8 ✓

Unit 2

2A

1

a 2 It's 3 She's 4 They're not 5 He's 6 it's not 7 It's 8 they are

2

a 2 your 3 his 4 their 5 my 6 her

3

a 2 c 3 a 4 e 5 b 6 d 7 g

b 2 right 3 difficult 4 good 5 happy 6 beautiful 7 easy 8 boring 9 interesting

4

a /h/: he, his, her, hello, who
/w/: where, what, when

2B

1

a 2 tickets 3 watches 4 bottles of water 5 knives 6 countries 7 boys 8 babies 9 houses 10 keys

2

a 2 I have two pens. 3 And do you have a dictionary? 4 Yes, I have a dictionary. 5 Timo, do you have a bottle of water? 6 But I have an apple!

3

a 2 book 3 keys 4 umbrella 5 phone 6 bottle

4

a 2 Thirty 3 six 4 Twelve 5 fifty 6 Fourteen

5

a /s/: students, tickets, books
/z/: keys, newspapers, bottles
/ɪz/: watches, houses

2C

1

a 2 spell 3 phone number 4 email address 5 first name

b 2 How do you spell that? 3 What's your address? 4 What's your phone number?

d 2 It's 3 How 4 What's 5 It's 6 address 7 It's

2

a 2 ↗ 3 ↘ 4 ↘ 5 ↗ 6 ↘ 7 ↗ 8 ↗ 9 ↘ 10 ↘

2C Skills for Writing

1

a 2 Stewart 3 American 4 745 5 Gem 6 Office 7 9178

2

a 2 F 3 G 4 O 5 X

b 2 spell 3 easy 4 phone 5 address 6 town 7 happy 8 nationality 9 office 10 email

3

a Sample answer:

First name: Sandro
Last name: Alessi
Nationality: Italian
Home address: 552 Old Town Street, Vancouver
Phone number: (604) 555-5687
Email: salessi93@travelmail.com

Reading and listening extension

1

a 4

b 2 a 3 b 4 b 5 b 6 a 7 a 8 a

2

a 1 one desk 2 three desks 3 two desks

b 1 b 2 c 3 a

c Darren: phone, newspaper, keys
Paula: laptop, bag, umbrella
Jamie: knife, glass of water

Review

1

2 I have three watches.
3 It's a beautiful town.
4 Beijing is a big city.
5 This is Kira and Paul, and this is their house.
6 My apartment is in an old part of town. It's very small.
7 Where's Anna? This is her bag.
8 Where are the knives?

2

2 small bottles of water
3 thirteen apartments
4 an interesting city
5 twelve phones
6 beautiful houses
7 an old umbrella
8 funny books

Unit 3

3A

1

a 2 Do you eat 3 don't eat 4 I don't 5 Do you like 6 don't 7 don't like 8 do

c 2 don't eat 3 you eat 4 don't 5 Do you 6 do 7 like

2

a 2 juice 3 eggs 4 soda 5 fruit 6 milk 7 meat 8 tea 9 bread 10 vegetables 11 rice 12 coffee

b Across: 3 meat 5 eggs 6 coffee 8 rice 10 bread 11 water
Down: 2 vegetables 4 tea 7 fish 9 soda

3

a /i/: tea, we, meat, key
/ɪ/: this, milk, is, Italy
/aɪ/: rice, I, like

3B

1

a 2 never eat 3 usually have 4 always have 5 sometimes eat 6 never have

b 2 always eat 3 sometimes eat 4 never have 5 usually have 6 always have

2

a 2 a cookie 3 tomato 4 An egg sandwich 5 pizza 6 orange

3

a 2 after 3 eleven 4 quarter 5 thirty 6 quarter 7 to 8 one

4

a /æ/: afternoon, half, past, class, banana
/ɔ/: four, store

3C

1

a 2 cake 3 go 4 water 5 pizza 6 course

b 2 Can I have a large coffee? 3 No, thanks. 4 OK. Thank you very much.

d 2 eat 3 I'd like 4 can I 5 of water 6 you go

2

a 2 b 3 a 4 b 5 a 6 a 7 b 8 a

3C Skills for Writing

1

a True: 1, 2, 4; False: 3, 5, 6

2

a 2 She is not 3 He is 4 We do not 5 They are not 6 It is

b 1 They're 2 we're, You're not / You aren't 3 don't 4 we're, It's 5 I'm, He's not 6 I'm not

3

a Sample answer:

Hi Liam,

I'm in New York. It's a great city! I'm very happy. I'm not at work. I'm in a café with my new friends Rafael and Inez. They're really nice.

Speak soon,
Brett

Reading and listening extension

1

a 2 coffee 3 like 4 three 5 don't have 6 evening

b True: 4, 6, 7; False: 1, 2, 3, 5, 8

2

a egg, chocolate, ice cream, tea, fruit juice

b Anna: 2, 5, 7, 8; John: 3, 4, 6

Review

1

2 ✓
3 We sometimes have pizza.
4 ✓
5 ✓
6 I don't like cheese.
7 Do you like meat?
8 They usually eat pizza for lunch.

2

2 ✓
3 We eat rice for lunch every day.
4 ✓
5 I never eat cookies.
6 We have breakfast at 7:30 a.m.
7 ✓
8 That sandwich is really big!

Unit 4

4A

1

a 2 Where's your apartment? 3 What do you eat for lunch? 4 What are their names? 5 Where do you study? 6 When does she start work?

b 2 do 3 is 4 do 5 are 6 is 7 are 8 do

2

a 2 b 3 a 4 b 5 c 6 a

b Across: 2 go 4 speak 5 teach 6 play
Down: 3 meet 4 study 7 live

3

a 2 Do you speak French? 3 Do you work in a factory? 4 What do you study?
5 Do you go to the gym? 6 When do you have lunch?

4B

1

a 2 teaches 3 lives 4 works 5 studies 6 plays 7 speaks 8 goes

b 2 goes 3 studies 4 has 5 drinks 6 teaches 7 works 8 lives

2

a 27 twenty-seven 45 forty-five 89 eighty-nine 34 thirty-four
98 ninety-eight 66 sixty-six 100 a hundred 72 seventy-two

3

a 2 father 3 mother 4 parents 5 brother 6 daughter 7 son 8 wife
9 sister

4

a 2, 4, 5, 7, 8, 10

4C

1

a 2 I do 3 Can I see 4 This is 5 Who's 6 Great 7 It's

c 2 **HUGO** Yes, I do.
3 **JENNY** Can I see them?
4 **HUGO** Sure. This is my dad and my brother.
5 **JENNY** Nice picture!
6 **HUGO** And this is me with my mom and my sister.
7 **JENNY** They look great! Thank you.

2

a /tʃ/: question, cheap, child, picture, watch
/dʒ/: page, Japan, Germany, manager

4C Skills for Writing

1

a 2 big 3 Italy 4 computers 5 is 6 teacher 7 is from 8 are

2

a 2 a 3 a 4 b 5 b 6 b

b 2 They live in Ecuador.
3 I don't live here.
4 These are my children Ruben and Cara.
5 I have a small apartment in Mexico City.
6 My sister studies English at college.

3

a Sample answer:

This is me with my friends Maria and Rob. They're married. We're at their house. It's a new house. It's big, and it's really nice! Maria teaches young children, and Rob is the manager of a café. He's very funny.

Reading and listening extension

1

a 2 c 3 a 4 f 5 b 6 d

b 2 Tom 3 Keiko 4 Daniel 5 Claire 6 Greg 7 Rei 8 Jeff

2

a 2 working at a university 3 language lessons 4 a vacation 5 parents

b 2 Philip 3 Philip 4 Kerry 5 Philip 6 Kerry 7 Kerry 8 Philip's

Review

1

2 He works in the Bahamas.
3 She has two brothers.
4 What's your name?
5 Her husband goes to work in the evening.
6 My sister studies German.
7 Where do you live?
8 Where are you from?

2

2 Our English class has six women and two men.
3 ✓
4 My sister is twenty-five years old.
5 ✓
6 Their son is thirty-three and their daughter is thirty-five.
7 His mother is a hundred years old.
8 I meet interesting people at work.

Unit 5

5A

1

a 2 There are two teachers. 3 There are a few cars. 4 There's a small museum.
5 There are ten families. 6 There's an old hospital.

c 2 There's 3 There's 4 There are 5 There are 6 There's 7 There are
8 There's

2

a /uː/: supermarket, school, beautiful, pool, who
/ʌ/: butter, sometimes, study, love, funny, mother

3

a 2 café 3 school 4 bank 5 restaurant 6 hotel 7 beach 8 park
9 swimming pool 10 bus stop 11 movie theater 12 hospital

5B

1

a 2 b 3 b 4 b 5 a 6 a

b 2 isn't 3 is 4 aren't any 5 There's a 6 Is there 7 Are there any
8 aren't 9 are

2

a 2, 4, 5, 6, 8, 10, 11

3

a 2 blanket 3 Wi-Fi 4 shower 5 room 6 towel 7 parking 8 pillow

b Across: 3 parking 4 towel 6 shower
Down: 1 blanket 2 TV 3 pillows 5 Wi-Fi 7 rooms

5C

1

a 2 there 3 near 4 There's 5 It's

b 2 Is there a movie theater near here?
3 OK. And is there a museum near here?
4 Oh yes! Great! Thanks for your help.

d 2 course 3 near 4 next 5 any 6 sorry 7 for 8 No

2

a 2 a 3 a 4 b 5 b 6 b 7 a 8 b

5C Skills for Writing

1

a True: 3, 4, 6, 7; False: 1, 2, 5, 8

2

a 2 a 3 a 4 a 5 a 6 b

b 2 but 3 but 4 but 5 and 6 and 7 but 8 but

3

a Sample answer:

Hi Marco,
I'm at the hotel. It's very old, but the room is very big (and it has Wi-Fi). There isn't a bathtub, but the shower is good, and there's a lot of hot water. The name of the hotel is Beach Hotel, but it's near the train station and a big movie theater. There aren't any stores, but there's a café and two restaurants. The restaurants are expensive, but the café is very cheap and good.
See you soon,
Sasha

Reading and listening extension

1

a 3, 4, 7, 8, 9, 10

b 2 Elam 3 Holly Road 4 Broadway Avenue 5 Clarkson Road 6 museum 7 ice cream shop 8 offices

2

a True: 1, 4; False: 2, 3

b Hotel Splendor: expensive, free Wi-Fi, rooms with bathtubs, TVs in rooms, free breakfast
Star Hostel: café, cheap, friendly, small clean rooms, near the train station, rooms with showers

c 2 one person 3 beach 4 $160 5 $40 6 first 7 two 8 Yusef

Review

1

2 There are two movie theaters.
3 ✓
4 ✓
5 No, there aren't.
6 ✓
7 Yes, there is.
8 There aren't any stores here.

2

2 Where's the school?
3 Is there a swimming pool?
4 Can I have a blanket, please?
5 There isn't a pillow on the bed.
6 Where's the hospital?
7 We often go to the beach.
8 Do you have a towel?

Unit 6

6A

1

a 2 don't 3 meet 4 don't 5 doesn't 6 like 7 don't 8 doesn't

b 2 don't teach 3 doesn't like 4 doesn't live 5 don't work 6 doesn't go 7 don't know 8 doesn't speak

2

a 2 factory worker 3 chef 4 server 5 soccer player 6 doctor 7 student 8 sales assistant 9 receptionist 10 office worker

b 2 businessman 3 worker 4 driver 5 chef 6 player 7 bank teller 8 doctor

3

a 2 a 3 b 4 b 5 a

6B

1

a 2 Where does Eduardo work?
3 What time does Richard wake up?
4 How does Amy feel after work?
5 Does Carol have breakfast at home?
6 What does your sister do at work?

b 2 Does 3 Martin get 4 does she 5 do Kathy 6 he does

2

a 2 get up 3 go to work 4 start work 5 have lunch 6 finish work 7 have dinner 8 go to bed

b 1 get 2 have 3 go 4 start, finish 5 arrive 6 go

3

a 2 breakfast 3 Spanish 4 play 5 fruit 6 class

6C

1

a 2 would you 3 that's OK 4 come 5 That's 6 I'll 7 that's

c 2 **RAUL** Yes, please.
3 **UMA** And would you like a piece of cake?
4 **RAUL** No, I'm fine, thanks – just coffee, please.
5 **UMA** I need to make lunch for José and Karina.
6 **RAUL** I'll help you.
7 **UMA** All right. Thanks. We need pizzas.
8 **RAUL** I can make pizzas. I make very good pizzas!
9 **UMA** Don't worry. It's OK. The pizzas at the supermarket are fine.
10 **RAUL** OK, I'll go to the supermarket.
11 **UMA** Thank you. That's great.

2

a 2 b 3 a 4 a 5 b 6 b

6C Skills for Writing

1

a 2 c 3 c 4 a 5 c 6 b

2

a 2 They have breakfast at school. They also have lunch at school.
3 I study business at college. I am also a server.
4 She gets up early. She also goes to bed early.
5 He gets up early because he's a teacher.
6 She sometimes works at night because she's a doctor.

b 2 because 3 also 4 because 5 because 6 also

3

a Sample answer:

My friend Alex is a soccer player. He plays soccer every day. He likes his job a lot, but it isn't easy. He gets up at 6:30 a.m. every day and goes to the gym from 7:00 a.m. until 8:00 a.m. He has breakfast at home. Alex starts soccer practice at 10:30 a.m. He finishes work at 12:00 p.m., and he has lunch at work with the other soccer players. He also plays soccer from 2:30 to 4:30 on Saturday afternoons. He doesn't work in the evening. He usually has dinner at home, but sometimes he goes to a restaurant. Alex often meets his friends and goes to the movies.

Reading and listening extension

1

a 1 on the weekend 2 in the morning 3 in the afternoon 4 in the evening 5 at night

b True: 2, 4, 6, 7; False: 1, 3, 5, 8

2

a 2 businessman 3 married 4 Detroit 5 Ninety 6 Canada

b 2 doesn't make 3 works 4 doesn't sit 5 meets 6 have 7 speaks 8 doesn't go

Review

1

2 Does he speak English?
3 When does Anna arrive home?
4 Does Pedro like fish?
5 Seb doesn't play tennis.
6 Yes, she does.
7 No, he doesn't.
8 Where does she live?

2

2 ✓
3 She's a taxi driver.
4 I have lunch at work.
5 He's a businessman.
6 ✓
7 ✓
8 I go to bed at 11:00 p.m.

Unit 7

7A

1

a 1 these 2 those 3 that 4 this

c 2 These 3 this 4 that 5 this 6 Those 7 that 8 these

2

a 2 plate 3 glass 4 suitcase 5 picture 6 book 7 guitar 8 speakers 9 plant 10 ball

3

a 2 c 3 b 4 a 5 b 6 a

4

a 2 suitcase 3 glass 4 bag 5 plate 6 lamp 7 guitar 8 book 9 cup 10 plant

7B

1

a 2 They're Darren's shoes. 3 My friend's jacket is brown. 4 The boys' pants are new. / The boy's pants are new. 5 I never wear jeans. 6 I sometimes wear my sister's clothes. / Sometimes I wear my sister's clothes.

c 2 Mehmet's 3 Juan and Laura's 4 the girls' 5 Sofia's 6 the children's

2

a 2 brown 3 yellow 4 white 5 red 6 green 7 black 8 blue

b Across: 3 pants 5 dark 6 gray 7 blouse 9 white
Down: 2 t(-)shirt 4 fashion 8 shoes

3

a /ʃ/: fashion, shoes, nationality, shirt, sure, shop
/dʒ/: large, Japanese, vegetables, Germany, gym

7C

1

a 2 No, thank you. Can I look around? 3 Here's your receipt. 4 How much are these bags? 5 I'd like that T-shirt, please.

c 2 **CUSTOMER** Yes, how much are these white shirts?
3 **SALES ASSISTANT** They're $4 each.
4 **CUSTOMER** OK, I'd like four white shirts, please.
5 **SALES ASSISTANT** Sure. That's $16, please.
6 **CUSTOMER** Can I pay with a card?
7 **SALES ASSISTANT** Of course. Enter your PIN, please. OK, here's your receipt. Would you like a bag?
8 **CUSTOMER** No, that's OK.
9 **SALES ASSISTANT** OK, here you go.
10 **CUSTOMER** Thank you very much.
11 **SALES ASSISTANT** Thank you.

2

a 2 /w/ 3 /j/ 4 /w/ 5 /j/ 6 /j/ 7 /j/ 8 /w/

7C Skills for Writing

1

a 2 C 3 D 4 B 5 A 6 C

2

a 2 b 3 c 4 c 5 b 6 a 7 c 8 a

b 2 You're a grandmother!
3 I have a sandwich, a drink, and a banana.
4 These shoes are very expensive!
5 Where is the bus stop?
6 Satako, Carolina, and Beto are in my class.

3

a Sample answer:

Hi Jason,
I saw your advertisement online for things you want to sell. I have a new house and I need four chairs, two tables, and a clock. How much are these things? Can I pay online with a credit card?
I also need a TV and a computer. How old is each item? How much is each item?
Thanks!
Rachel

Reading and listening extension

1

a a 2 b 4 c 3 d 1

b True: 1, 2, 5, 7; False: 3, 4, 6, 8

2

a things for the home

b 4, 5, 7, 9

c 2 useful 3 animals 4 brown 5 color 6 laptop 7 $60 8 card store

Review

1

2 These cups are $6.
3 ✓
4 That picture is interesting.
5 I like Martin's shoes.
6 ✓
7 ✓
8 It's Anna and David's computer.

2

2 He has a red guitar.
3 This picture is one hundred and sixty-three dollars.
4 Do you have any speakers?
5 It's a light brown skirt.
6 Where's your green jacket?
7 I have six white shirts.
8 It's a dark gray coat.

Unit 8

8A

1

a 2 Where was Nina this morning? 3 We weren't at the concert last night. 4 They were in Bogotá a week ago. 5 Were you in Mexico City last week? 6 Yes, we were. 7 Was Adrian at the meeting this afternoon? 8 No, he wasn't.

b 2 were 3 was 4 were 5 was 6 wasn't 7 were 8 were 9 Was 10 was 11 were 12 wasn't

2

a 2 Yesterday 3 this afternoon 4 this morning 5 last night 6 last month

c 2 yesterday 3 this 4 last 5 last night 6 three months ago

3

a 2 We were in Quito. 3 You were at work. 4 My parents were in Italy. 5 The party was fun. 6 The game was exciting. 7 The concert was good. 8 The meetings were interesting.

8B

1

a Across: 2 saw 4 looked 5 watched 8 came 9 ate 10 had
Down: 1 jumped 3 walked 5 went 6 tried 7 heard 8 called

b 2 watched 3 played 4 tried 5 went 6 saw 7 said 8 heard 9 talked 10 stayed 11 had 12 played

2

a 2 listen to 3 take 4 go 5 have 6 read 7 play 8 watch 9 go

b 2 watch 3 go 4 read 5 take 6 listen to 7 watch 8 play 9 listen to 10 go

3

a 2 /d/ 3 /d/ 4 /d/ 5 /d/ 6 /t/ 7 /t/ 8 /d/

8C

1

a 2 Let's 3 Do you want 4 free 5 could

b 2 That's 3 could 4 busy 5 Do 6 can't 7 free 8 OK

d 2 **ANYA** Coffee? Good idea!
3 **SAYEED** Great! Let's go now.
4 **ANYA** I'm sorry, I can't go now. I have a meeting at ten o'clock.
5 **SAYEED** OK. We could go at eleven.
6 **ANYA** Great! Do you want to go to the new Italian café?
7 **SAYEED** OK, that's a nice idea! See you at eleven.

2

a 2 ↘ 3 ↘ 4 ↗ 5 ↘ 6 ↘

8C Skills for Writing

1

a 2 Oscar 3 Emi 4 Russell 5 Elena 6 Nina

2

a 2 want 3 for 4 was 5 I hope 6 Here are 7 See

b 2 a 3 f 4 e 5 b 6 c

3

a Sample answer:

Hi Maria,
I want to say thank you for lunch on Sunday. The food was great. I liked the fish, and the chocolate cake was really good. It was great to meet your brothers. Andy's very interesting, and Martin's very funny! Here are some photos of Martin with the fish and Andy in the yard. I hope we can meet again soon.
Talk to you later!
Chris

Reading and listening extension

1

a True: 1, 2, 4; False: 3, 5, 6

b 2 stayed at home 3 tired 4 watched a cooking show 5 a suitcase 6 dinner 7 four 8 early 9 9:30 10 for vacation

2

a 2 work 3 a concert 4 the park 5 San Diego 6 a restaurant 7 the beach 8 a museum

b Grace: 2, 5, 7, 8, 10
Matt: 3, 4, 6, 9

Review

1

2 Emilia wasn't at work yesterday.
3 We were in the U.S. in 2018.
4 Where were they yesterday?
5 We played tennis.
6 Jessie arrived at nine o'clock.
7 I had breakfast this morning.
8 Carrie went to New York last year.

2

2 I saw Jeff last week.
3 ✓
4 ✓
5 They listened to music last night.
6 ✓
7 ✓
8 We went to the movies yesterday.

Unit 9

9A

1

a 2 didn't stay 3 didn't meet 4 didn't drive 5 didn't go 6 didn't cook

b 2 didn't visit 3 didn't go 4 didn't drive 5 didn't buy 6 didn't read

2

a 2 plane 3 bike 4 car 5 subway 6 taxi 7 train 8 bus 9 boat

3

a /æ/: taxi, tram, bag, camp
/ɑ/: car, father, garden, watch
/eɪ/: train, take, plane

9B

1

a 2 How did you get there? 3 Did you go with a friend? 4 Where did you stay? 5 What time did you get up? 6 Did you buy a lot of things? 7 Did you go to the beach? 8 Did you enjoy your trip?

b 2 Did you 3 I didn't 4 did you stay 5 Did Jack stay 6 he didn't 7 Did he 8 he did 9 did he get 10 was

2

a

r	a	i	n	y	j	x	l	y	s
z	y	v	p	x	l	z	z	p	p
f	w	a	r	m	j	q	c	k	r
f	y	p	n	b	h	v	o	d	i
y	j	a	q	k	o	x	l	x	n
c	l	u	s	k	t	v	d	d	g
l	b	t	j	z	h	q	t	p	p
o	f	u	q	s	u	m	m	e	r
u	b	m	v	n	k	t	l	v	z
d	q	n	n	j	p	y	f	t	s
y	x	b	v	t	j	z	y	k	n
q	w	i	n	t	e	r	v	q	o
y	p	s	u	n	n	y	z	j	w

b 2 cold 3 snow 4 windy 5 wind 6 rain 7 rains 8 hot 9 warm 10 sunny

3

a /oʊ/: snowy, cold, phone, ago
/aʊ/: town, brown, how
/ɑ/: hot, shopping, doctor, wrong

9C

1

a 2 Oh, OK, I'll do it then.
3 Can you do something for me?
4 Could you meet me at the bus station on Sunday?
5 Thanks, that's really nice of you.
6 Sorry, I can't. I'm really busy.
7 Sure, no problem.

c 2 **SAÚL** Hi Karina, how are you?
3 **KARINA** I'm good, thanks. Could you do something for me?
4 **SAÚL** Yes, of course. What is it?
5 **KARINA** Can you pick Jenny up from school at four?
6 **SAÚL** Sure, no problem.
7 **KARINA** Thanks, that's really nice of you.
8 **SAÚL** Any time. See you later.
9 **KARINA** See you later.

2

a 2 syllables: station, every, different, camera, favorite, business
3 syllables: museum, interesting, vegetable, difficult

9C Skills for Writing

1

a 2 Jiang, Fernanda 3 Jiang, Fernanda 4 Luke, Fernanda 5 Jiang, Luke 6 Luke 7 Jiang 8 Jiang, Luke, Fernanda

2

a 2 Then, 3 After that, 4 After that, 5 then 6 First, 7 Then, 8 After that,

3

a Sample answer:

Last New Year's Eve, I went to two parties. First, I went to my friend Katherine's house. It wasn't a big party, but it was very fun. I didn't stay late because Katherine and her husband have three small children. Next, I drove to a party in a different town. The weather was really bad. It was cold, windy, and very rainy. This party was big and exciting. There was a lot of good food and music. At 12:00 a.m., my friends and I went into the yard. We saw some fireworks. After that, I went home.

Reading and listening extension

1

a Billy 2 Monica 3 Lucio 1

b 2 Monica 3 Billy 4 Lucio 5 Billy 6 Monica 7 Monica 8 Lucio

2

a 2 doesn't know 3 on the street today 4 man's

b 2 He went on vacation with his wife.
3 ✓
4 They were on vacation for three weeks.
5 They stayed in a house near the beach.
6 It was their second visit to Miami.
7 Dan learned some Spanish phrases on his vacation.
8 ✓

Review

1

2 ✓
3 I didn't see Sabine.
4 What time did you arrive?
5 ✓
6 ✓
7 **B** No, I didn't.
8 ✓

2

2 We took the train to Milan. / We took a train to Milan.
3 We went by plane to Cuenca. / We flew to Cuenca. / We took a plane to Cuenca.
4 This is a photo of the snow in the garden.
5 **B** No, we went by bus. / No, we took the bus.
6 It always rains here in the summer. / It's always rainy here in the summer.
7 Did you go by car to Medellín? / Did you drive to Medellín?
8 It was sunny and warm yesterday.

Unit 10

10A

1

a 2 Jaime's listening 3 It's raining, 4 We're having 5 I'm looking, It's sitting

b 2 's drinking 3 're going 4 'm working 5 's wearing 6 're studying

2

a Across: 2 bathroom 4 dining room 5 living room 6 window 7 floor
Down: 2 bedroom 3 door 6 wall

3

a /tʃ/: kitchen, picture, chair, question
/θ/: ninth, month, thirty

10B

1

a 2 We're not studying. 3 Why is Ryan talking on the phone?
4 I'm not reading this book. 5 Are your friends waiting for the bus?
6 Erica's not staying at the hotel.

c 2 are you working 3 are you talking 4 I'm not talking 5 I'm talking
6 's not listening 7 we're not working

2

a 2 at 3 at 4 on 5 at 6 on 7 on 8 at 9 in 10 at 11 at 12 at

b 1 **B** at 2 **A** at **B** on 3 **A** at **B** in 4 **A** at **B** in 5 **A** on **B** in 6 **A** at **B** on

3

a 2 picture 3 Brazil 4 daughter 5 autumn 6 ago 7 woman 8 correct
9 computer 10 afternoon

10C

1

a 2 office 3 train 4 ten minutes 5 four o'clock 6 stop

b 2 can 3 next 4 at 5 direct 6 change 7 bus stop 8 ticket 9 help
10 problem

d 2 **B** Yes? How can I help?
3 **A** What time's the next train to Cleveland?
4 **B** The next train leaves in half an hour.
5 **A** So at 10:25. Is it a direct train?
6 **B** No, you change at Cincinnati.
7 **A** OK, and which platform is it?
8 **B** It's platform 9.
9 **A** Great! Thanks for your help.
10 **B** No problem.

2

a /ɪə/: we're, zero, really, here, clear
/eə/: wear, yeah, chair, where

10C Skills for Writing

1

a True: 2, 5; False: 1, 3, 4, 6

2

a 2 Is the train 3 is he going 4 did you buy 5 does the movie start
6 can, get 7 Is it an expensive 8 Does the hotel have

b 2 Is Nick playing on the computer?
3 How many rooms does their apartment have?
4 Did the teacher give us any homework yesterday?
5 Where can I buy a bus ticket?
6 Was he at school today?

3

a Sample answer:

Hi Eduardo. Right now I'm on the bus going to our English class. Sorry, I can't remember three things. Where is the new classroom? What time does class start? And did we have any homework? Thanks! See you soon!

Reading and listening extension

1

a 2 ✓
3 There are four people in the German family.
4 Today is Sunday.
5 ✓
6 Most people in the family are inside now.
7 Anna wants to know what Jenny is doing.

b 2 two-week 3 a house 4 understand 5 Karl 6 playing a game 7 working
8 music

2

a 2 Dad 3 Gloria 4 Mom, Tim / Tim, Mom

b 2 at home 3 listening to music 4 aren't 5 one of her sons 6 coat
7 snow 8 is

Review

1

2 She isn't working today.
3 Are you having lunch?
4 Where's Elena going?
5 They're sitting in the yard.
6 Is it raining?
7 No, it isn't.
8 Yes, it is.

2

2 ✓
3 I'm in the kitchen.
4 ✓
5 ✓
6 They're in the dining room.
7 ✓
8 Jorge isn't in bed.
9 I'm at the airport.
10 We're in a taxi.

Unit 11

11A

1

a 2 We, us 3 I, her 4 me 5 it 6 He, him 7 you

b 2 They 3 them 4 He 5 he 6 him 7 He 8 It 9 you 10 me
11 They 12 She 13 She 14 us 15 her 16 She 17 you

2

a 2 grow up 3 finish college 4 stop working 5 be born 6 go to school 7 die 8 go to college 9 have a baby

b 2 went to 3 had 4 up 5 school 6 college 7 died 8 stopped 9 got

3

a 1 17 2 30 3 90 4 16 5 50 6 18

11B

1

a 2 **A** Can you **B** I can 3 can't 4 can 5 **A** Can he **B** can't 6 can swim very well

c 2 can't swim 3 can read 4 Can, drive 5 can't teach 6 can say 7 can write 8 can't play

2

a 2 e 3 c 4 b 5 g 6 d 7 a 8 h

c Across: 2 played 6 ran 7 cooked 8 painted
Down: 1 swam 3 danced 4 rode 5 drove

3

a 2 b 3 b 4 a 5 a 6 a

11C

1

a 2 right 3 idea 4 nice 5 think 6 agree 7 favorite

b 2 think 3 Maybe you're 4 I 5 so 6 did 7 I agree 8 think so

d 2 think 3 so 4 don't 5 right 6 did

2

a 2 engineer, enjoy 3 answer, dance 4 school, ask 5 think, bank 6 listened, find 7 clocks, six 8 interesting, paint

11C Skills for Writing

1

a 2 a 3 c 4 c 5 a 6 b

2

a 2 They 3 It's 4 It's 5 She's 6 her 7 him 8 we 9 them 10 you

3

a Sample answer:

Hi Jaime,
Thanks for your email. I'm in Miami at the moment. I'm studying English at a small language school in downtown Miami. It's going OK, but it's pretty difficult for me to learn all the new words. The pronunciation is also difficult, but the classes are always fun because the teacher's very good. His name's Jeff, and he's from Ohio.

There are nine students in my class. We all come from different countries. We usually meet for coffee in the morning. It's a good time to practice English.

Goodbye for now.
Write soon!
Fabián

Reading and listening extension

1

a 4, 6, 7, 8

b 2 She got a job in New York City. 3 She finished college. 4 She got married. 5 She had a baby. 6 Her husband died. 7 She went to Haiti. 8 She started teaching.

2

a 2 chef 3 English teacher 4 receptionist 5 tour guide

b 4, 6

c 2 an office 3 Camila 4 two jobs 5 Spanish 6 hot 7 knows 8 Boston

Review

1

2 Your dad's an engineer. We could ask him for help.
3 Is your phone new? I like it.
4 Your sister's really nice. How often do you see her?
5 He can ride a horse.
6 Can you drive?
7 I can't sing.
8 **B** Yes, they can.

2

2 I was born in 1995.
3 She died in 2002.
4 I finished college last year.
5 I grew up in a small town in Ecuador.
6 My father stopped working last year.
7 She sang a song last week.
8 I drove the car to the train station.
9 I ran 10 km last Saturday.
10 We swam in the new swimming pool yesterday.

Unit 12

12A

1

a 2 I'm not going to 3 to call 4 I'm going to 5 I'm going 6 are going 7 are going 8 She isn't going

c 2 is going to cook 3 am not going to sing 4 is going to do 5 aren't going to stay 6 isn't going to ride 7 am going to take 8 are going to watch 9 aren't going to use

2

a 2 b 3 b 4 c 5 a 6 a 7 b 8 a 9 c 10 c

3

a 2nd second 3rd third 4th fourth 5th fifth 9th ninth 12th twelfth 13th thirteenth 16th sixteenth 20th twentieth 22nd twenty-second 31st thirty-first

4

a 2 They're going to <u>live</u> in <u>Canada</u>.
3 <u>Anna's</u> going to <u>do</u> her <u>homework</u>.
4 I'm going to <u>check</u> my <u>email</u>.
5 He's going to <u>listen</u> to <u>music</u>.
6 I'm going to <u>read</u> a <u>book</u>.

12B

1

a 2 Is he going to have lunch at home?
3 Where are they going to get married?
4 Are you going to drive to the train station tomorrow?
5 What's she going to do this evening?
6 How are you going to cook the potatoes?

c 1 **B** 'm going to clean, 're going to help
2 **A** is he going to play **B** Are you going to listen
3 **A** are you and your friends going to do **B** 're going to talk
4 's she going to watch
5 am I going to do

2

a 2 a 3 e 4 d 5 b 6 g 7 c 8 f

b Across: 2 play 5 shopping 8 invite 10 start
Down: 3 visit 4 go 6 paint 7 use 9 make

3

a /v/: evening, visit, November, volleyball, drive, invite
/w/: Wi-Fi, warm, windy, winter, weekend

12C

1

a 2 **B** I'd like to, but I have a lot of homework for tomorrow.
3 **A** You're a good student! Are you free tomorrow night?
4 **B** Yes, I am.
5 **A** Great! Then do you want to go see a movie?
6 **B** Sure, that sounds like fun. Thank you.

c 2 **B** Sorry, I'm busy then.
3 **A** Are you free on Friday?
4 **B** No, sorry, I'm busy on Friday too. But Saturday's OK.
5 **A** Great! You can come on Saturday.
6 **B** Thanks!

e 2 sounds 3 Do 4 busy 5 OK 6 can 7 go 8 to 9 free 10 Thank

2

a /uː/: pool, school, food, boots, afternoon
/ʊ/: good, cook, look

12C Skills for Writing

1

a True: 1, 4, 8; False: 2, 3, 5, 6, 7

2

a 1 Hi Juan,
2 I'm thinking about having a barbecue at my house on Saturday evening – chicken, fish, vegetables, things like that. Would you and Ada like to come?
3 Paul's staying with me this week, and he can play the guitar really well. We could eat and then sing songs. What do you think? Are you free on Saturday?
4 I hope you can come!
5 Ethan

b 1 Hi Ethan,
2 Thank you, that sounds great. We're busy on Saturday afternoon, but we can come in the evening.
3 Is 8:00 OK? Would you like us to bring some food?
4 See you on Saturday!
5 Juan

3

a Sample answer:

Hi Hector!
Thanks, I'd like to come, but I'm busy on Saturday. I'm at work in the morning, and I'm going to watch my brother in a basketball game in the afternoon. But I'm free on Sunday, and Oliver and Jorge are always free on Sundays. What do you think? Is Sunday OK for you?

Reading and listening extension

1

a a 4 b 5 c 3 d 1 e 2

b 3, 7, 9, 10, 11

2

a Fernanda: see a soccer game, spend a day at Disneyland
Bruno: take the dog for a walk, have dinner, read a book
Mom: meet friends, go to the movies
Dad: play tennis

b True: 1, 2, 5, 7; False: 3, 4, 6, 8

Review

1

2 They're going to play volleyball. Do you want to watch them?
3 ✓
4 What are we going to do now?
5 **B** Yes, he is.
6 ✓
7 I'm not going to get up early. I'm going to stay in bed until lunchtime!
8 When am I going to see you again?

2

2 They're going to visit João in the summer.
3 It's August twelfth.
4 I'm going to start work on Monday.
5 He was born on February fifteenth.
6 My clothes are dirty. I need to do laundry.
7 We could invite Leo and Craig to the party. They love parties!
8 I don't really like to play sports, but I do yoga every day.
9 I want to paint the walls green.
10 Can I use the computer for five minutes? I need to check my email.

Acknowledgments

The authors and publishers acknowledge the following sources of copyright material and are grateful for the permissions granted. While every effort has been made, it has not always been possible to identify the sources of all the material used, or to trace all copyright holders. If any omissions are brought to our notice, we will be happy to include the appropriate acknowledgments on reprinting and in the next update to the digital edition, as applicable.

Key:
U = Unit

Photographs
All the photographs are sourced from Getty Images.
Front cover photography by Don Mason/Getty Images.
U1: RichVintage/E+; Anastasiia_M/iStock/Getty Images Plus; Clasos/LatinContent Editorial; Patrik Giardino/Stone; Morsa Images/DigitalVision; JohnnyGreig/E+; YurolaitsAlbert/iStock/Getty Images Plus; Visualspace/E+; **U2:** Grace Cary/Moment; Urbancow/iStock/Getty Images Plus; Yacobchuk/iStock/Getty Images Plus; laflor/E+; DianeBentleyRaymond/iStock/Getty Images Plus; Darwin Fan/Moment; Westend61; **U3:** PeopleImages/iStock/Getty Images Plus; Radionphoto/iStock/Getty Images Plus; Caiaimage; FangXiaNuo/iStock/Getty Images Plus; Creativeye99/iStock/Getty Images Plus; Hispanolistic/E+; LauriPatterson/E+; **U4:** YAndresr/E+; Shapecharge/E+; Monkeybusinessimages/iStock/Getty Images Plus; Jacob Rushing/Image Source; Virsuziglis/iStock/Getty Images Plus; **U5:** IPGGutenbergUKLtd/iStock/Getty Images Plus; Andreka/iStock/Getty Images Plus; Monkeybusinessimages/iStock/Getty Images Plus; Patrick Foto/Moment; JackF/iStock/Getty Images Plus; Hispanolistic/E+; Awl Images; Eyeem; Miljko/E+; Monty Rakusen/Cultura; Aliraza Khatri's Photography/Moment; Jetta Productions Inc/The Image Bank/Getty Images Plus; Andresr/E+; Glenn van der Knijff/Lonely Planet Images/Getty Images Plus; CaronB/iStock/Getty Images Plus; Recep-bg/E+; **U6:** Vladimir Godnik; Milos Dimic/E+; Walter Lockwood/Photolibrary/Getty Images Plus; Michael Blann/DigitalVision; Mike Powell/Allsport Concepts/Getty Images Plus; Chabruken/Taxi/Getty Images Plus; Mediaphotos/E+; Ftwitty/E+; Cecilie_Arcurs/E+; Maskot; Pixelfit/E+; PeopleImages/E+; Stockvisual/E+; **U7:** Zoranm/E+; Daniela Duncan/Moment; BrianAJackson/iStock/Getty Images Plus; AdrianHancu/iStock/Getty Images Plus; Neyya/iStock/Getty Images Plus; **U8:** Noam Galai/noamgalai.com/Moment; Czekma13/iStock/Getty Images Plus; Doble.d/Moment Open; Wundervisuals/E+; Graffizone/E+; Dennis K. Johnson/Lonely Planet Images/Getty Images Plus; **U9:** Malorny/Moment; Jkristoffersson/iStock; Grafissimo/E+; Polina Chalaia/EyeEm; Car Culture; Georgeclerk/iStock; Bgwalker/iStock; New SIGHT Photography/iStock/Getty Images Plus; Tupungato/iStock Editorial/Getty Images Plus; Marcus Lindstrom/iStock/Getty Images Plus; J-wildman/iStock/Getty Images Plus; Alexander Spatari/Moment; Robert Daly/OJO Images; Paula Hible/Photolibrary/Getty Images Plus; Panya Kuanun/EyeEm; Mladn61/E+; George Pachantouris/Moment; Thomas Northcut/Photodisc; Patrick Keyser/Moment; Pigphoto/iStock/Getty Images Plus; Czekma13/iStock/Getty Images Plus; Allou/iStock/Getty Images Plus; **U10:** StockstudioX/E+; Westend61; Hill Street Studios/DigitalVision; Hero Images; Image Source/DigitalVision; Pixelfit/E+; FotoTravel/iStock/Getty Images Plus; Russell102/iStock/Getty Images Plus; Urbazon/E+; Paul Bradbury/OJO Images; JohnnyGreig/E+; **U11:** Nick David/Stone; _IB_/iStock/Getty Images Plus; Real444/E+; Fuse/Corbis; Dean Mitchell/E+; Photographer Nick Measures/Moment; Klaus Vedfelt/DigitalVision; Mark Williamson/Photodisc; Skynesher/E+; Vanessa Davies/Dorling Kindersley/Getty Images Plus; Vadimguzhva/iStock/Getty Images Plus; KatarzynaBialasiewicz/iStock/Getty Images Plus; Eric Audras/ONOKY; Angelo D'Amico/iStock/Getty Images Plus; Richcano/iStock/Getty Images Plus; Alvarez/E+; Val Thoermer/EyeEm; **U12:** Holger Leue/The Image Bank; Simonkr/E+; Valentyn Semenov/EyeEm; Mikkelwilliam/E+; Hispanolistic/E+.

The following photographs are sourced from other sources/libraries.

U1: Shutterstock/William Perugini; **U5**: Shutterstock/Andrey tiyk; **U12**: Shutterstock/ESB Professional.

Commissioned photography by Gareth Boden.

Illustrations
QBS Learning; Mark Bird; Mark Duffin; Sally Elford; John Goodwin (Eye Candy Illustration); Dusan Lakicevic (Beehive Illustration); Roger Penwill; Gavin Reece (New Division); Martin Sanders (Beehive Illustration); Sean 290 (KJA Artists); David Semple; Marie-Eve Tremblay (Colagene); Andrea Turvey (Eye Candy Illustration); Gary Venn (Lemonade Illustration).

Typeset by QBS Learning.

Audio Production by John Marshall Media.

Corpus
Development of this publication has made use of the Cambridge English Corpus (CEC). The CEC is a computer database of contemporary spoken and written English, which currently stands at over one billion words. It includes British English, American English, and other varieties of English. It also includes the Cambridge Learner Corpus, developed in collaboration with the University of Cambridge ESOL Examinations. Cambridge University Press has built up the CEC to provide evidence about language use that helps us to produce better language teaching materials.

English Profile
This product is informed by English Vocabulary Profile, built as part of English Profile, a collaborative program designed to enhance the learning, teaching, and assessment of English worldwide. Its main funding partners are Cambridge University Press and Cambridge Assessment English and its aim is to create a "profile" for English, linked to the Common European Framework of Reference for Languages (CEFR). English Profile outcomes, such as the English Vocabulary Profile, will provide detailed information about the language that learners can be expected to demonstrate at each CEFR level, offering a clear benchmark for learners' proficiency. For more information, please visit www.englishprofile.org.

CALD
The Cambridge Advanced Learner's Dictionary is the world's most widely used dictionary for learners of English. Including all the words and phrases that learners are likely to come across, it also has easy-to-understand definitions and example sentences to show how the word is used in context. The Cambridge Advanced Learner's Dictionary is available online at dictionary.cambridge.org.

CAMBRIDGE
UNIVERSITY PRESS

University Printing House, Cambridge CB2 8BS, United Kingdom

One Liberty Plaza, 20th Floor, New York, NY 10006, USA

477 Williamstown Road, Port Melbourne, VIC 3207, Australia

314–321, 3rd Floor, Plot 3, Splendor Forum, Jasola District Centre, New Delhi – 110025, India

103 Penang Road, #05-06/07, Visioncrest Commercial, Singapore 238467

Cambridge University Press is part of the University of Cambridge.

It furthers the University's mission by disseminating knowledge in the pursuit of education, learning and research at the highest international levels of excellence.

www.cambridge.org
Information on this title: www.cambridge.org/9781108818148

First published 2022

20 19 18 17 16 15 14 13 12 11 10 9 8 7 6 5 4 3 2

Printed in Italy by Rotolito S.p.A.

A catalogue record for this publication is available from the British Library

ISBN 978-1-108-81813-1 Starter Student's Book with eBook
ISBN 978-1-108-81831-5 Starter Student's Book A with eBook
ISBN 978-1-108-81832-2 Starter Student's Book B with eBook
ISBN 978-1-108-86221-9 Starter Student's Book with Digital Pack
ISBN 978-1-108-86227-1 Starter Student's Book A with Digital Pack
ISBN 978-1-108-86229-5 Starter Student's Book B with Digital Pack
ISBN 978-1-108-81814-8 Starter Workbook with Answers
ISBN 978-1-108-81815-5 Starter Workbook A with Answers
ISBN 978-1-108-81819-3 Starter Workbook B with Answers
ISBN 978-1-108-81820-9 Starter Workbook without Answers
ISBN 978-1-108-81825-4 Starter Workbook A without Answers
ISBN 978-1-108-81826-1 Starter Workbook B without Answers
ISBN 978-1-108-81827-8 Starter Full Contact with eBook
ISBN 978-1-108-81828-5 Starter Full Contact A with eBook
ISBN 978-1-108-81829-2 Starter Full Contact B with eBook
ISBN 978-1-108-86223-3 Starter Full Contact with Digital Pack
ISBN 978-1-108-86224-0 Starter Full Contact A with Digital Pack
ISBN 978-1-108-86225-7 Starter Full Contact B with Digital Pack
ISBN 978-1-108-81833-9 Starter Teacher's Book with Digital Pack
ISBN 978-1-108-81810-0 Starter Presentation Plus

Additional resources for this publication at www.cambridge.org/americanempower

This page is intentionally left blank.

This page is intentionally left blank.

This page is intentionally left blank.

This page is intentionally left blank.

This page is intentionally left blank.